Thank you

The Bible is inherent; it is part of the very nature of God and, therefore, permanently characteristic of or necessarily involved in it. It reveals His will, His love, and His plan for humanity. Creation tells of His will for good things for humanity. He gave His Son to prove His love. And His word points the way back to holy union and communion with Himself. "Blessed *is* he that reads, and they that hear the words of this prophecy, and keep those things which are written therein: for the time *is* at hand" (Rev. 1:3).

We are embarking on a journey from Origin back to Destiny. Consider this book as your personal lamp lighting your way of hope of eternal life. And be forewarned, for, as you read, "radical changes will occur within you." But I must ask, "Where will you spend your long eternity?" I dreamed I searched Heaven for you. Oh, won't you prepare to meet me up there? Maratha!

From Eden back to Eternity

Holy Warfare

Revised Edition

Rudolph A. Whyte

Copyright © 2013 by Rudolph A. Whyte.

Library of Congress Control Number:		2013922023
ISBN:	Hardcover	978-1-4931-4851-6
	Softcover	978-1-4931-4850-9
	eBook	978-1-4931-4852-3

All rights reserved. No part of this book may be reproduced or transmitted in any form or by any means, electronic or mechanical, including photocopying, recording, or by any information storage and retrieval system, without permission in writing from the copyright owner.

Scripture quotations are from the authorized King James Version of the Holy Bible.

This book was printed in the United States of America.

Rev. date: 1/31/2014

To order additional copies of this book, contact:
Xlibris LLC
1-888-795-4274
www.Xlibris.com
Orders@Xlibris.com

Contents

Special Thanks 7
Preface 9

1. The Perfect Praise 13
2. Satan's Beginning 19
3. The fall of Adam 26
4. The Curse 28
5. From Death Came Life 32
6. Pathway: Back to God and to Eden 35
7. The Keeper 38
8. Leaves Will Not Do 41
9. Only the Best Will Do 45
10. Satan's Engagement with Man 48
11. Bags of Burdens 53
12. The Temperament of Things 60
13. What in Hell Do You Want? 64
14. A Look into Hell 69
15. Death and Undying Penalty 71
16. The Last God (God of the flesh) 79
17. The Path Back to Eternity 84
18. Face-to-Face with God 90
19. Back to Eternity 94
20. God Cried 101

Notes 105

Special Thanks

Rev. Betty Cooper, who has supported me with her prayers and encouraging words, while audaciously lifting up my hands through the many difficult circumstances I had to face. As Caleb and Joshua held up Moses's hands, so has she demonstrated true love for the will of God in my life by holding up my hands. God sent her to me at a time when I needed her the most. I dub her "virtuous woman," born again for such a time as this. God will reward her for her faithfulness.

To Mrs. Denese Buchanan that was invariably eager to assist in the final preparation for publishing of this book: many thanks. May voluminous blessings from God the Father of our Lord Jesus Christ overtake you with lifelong joy and peace.

To all my friends for their encouraging words and prayers: may God ever keep you in His perfect will.

To my loving wife Angella, who has graciously borne the weight of my efforts without repining. Your appreciative love, support, prayers, patience, and understanding of the call of God in my life have helped me in many ways to complete the writing of this book.

Preface

Have you ever asked these questions: why did Adam fall? Did God make the Devil? Did Adam and Eve actually eat an apple? Is hell a place or a condition? Is Heaven a place or setting? The following pages contain answers to a number of these questions and more. Like a torch, the book lights the way you should take, to the written and living truths, making you free, and the high-status life of God's children traveling to Heaven.

You will be acquainted with God's plan for humanity, starting from Eden his birthplace and Eternity his Origin. Holy warfare and the path ordained for man's return. God dwells in Eternity, and He is the purpose of all things, whether of Heaven or of earth. Purpose is in the mind of the Creator. Apostle Paul wrote, "Blessed *be* the God and Father of our Lord Jesus Christ, who has blessed us with every spiritual blessing in the heavenly *places* in Christ, just as He chose us in Him before the foundation of the world, that we should be holy and without blame before Him in love, having predestined us to adoption as sons by Jesus Christ to Himself, according to the good pleasure of His will, to the praise of the glory of His grace, by which He made us accepted in the Beloved."

As you read, you will understand how and why the Almighty God revealed Himself to me, as He cried for souls—yes, God cried tears, impressing on my heart the need to reach the lost at any cost. Apostle Paul wrote again, "If the gospel is hid, it is hid to them that are lost," and in order to live victoriously over sin, the Body of Christ needs an awakening to the mysteries in the Word of God. In view of the fact that the Gospel truth is most times obscure, many are confused and cannot find their way to God.

The path back to fellowship with Him is set forth from Genesis to Revelation, and not many will find it. Knowledge is power, and knowing is half the battle.

"In Him we have redemption through His blood, the forgiveness of sins, according to the riches of His grace which He made to abound toward us in all wisdom and prudence, having made known to us the mystery of His will, according to His good pleasure which He purposed in Himself, that in the dispensation of the fullness of the times He might gather together in one all things in Christ, both which are in heaven and which are on earth. Even so, come Lord Jesus." Amen.

The Bible is inherent; it is part of the very nature of God and, therefore, permanently characteristic of or necessarily involved in it. It reveals His will, His love, and His plan for humanity. Creation tells of His will for good things for humanity. He gave His Son to prove His love. His Word points the way back to holy union and communion with Himself.

Jesus Christ was present from side to side in every dispensation, stipulating redemption. The pathway back to Eternity is identified in the course of His works throughout the Bible. Genesis portrays Him as the following: our Creator God, Exodus our Passover Lamb, Leviticus our Praise and Worship example, Numbers the Lifted-up one, Deuteronomy the Law-giver, Joshua the Captain of our salvation, Judges our Righteous Judge, Ruth our Kinsman Redeemer, 1 and 2 Samuel the true Prophet, 1 and 2 Kings the King of Kings, 1 and 2 Chronicles the Head of all tribes, Ezra our Lawyer, Nehemiah our Restorer, Esther our Deliverer, and Job our Stronghold in the day of calamity.

Psalms our All in All, Proverbs our Wisdom, Ecclesiastes our Sufficiency, Songs of Solomon the Lover of our souls, Isaiah our coming Messiah, Jeremiah He will marry the backslider, Lamentation the weeping Prophet, Ezekiel our Promise Keeper, Daniel the Smiting Stone, Hosea our Restorer, Joel and Amos the Judge against rebellious nations, Obadiah a Promise Keeper, and Jonah is a Forgiver of sins.

Matthew portrays Him as Christ Jehovah's King, Hebrews He is our Faith, and Jude He is able to keep you from falling and to present *you* faultless before the presence of His glory with exceeding joy. To the only Wise God our Savior *be* Glory and Majesty, Dominion and Power, both now and ever. Revelation He is our returning King of kings and Lord of lords. Amen.

Many dreams originate from God and through the abundance of inspired reflections of the Holy Spirit. However, we must become conscious to the fact that loads of thoughts and dreams do come about by human experiences, and demonic influences as Satan competes with the Spirit of God to gain our attention.

"In Him also we have obtained an inheritance, being predestined according to the purpose of Him who works all things according to the counsel of His will that we who first trusted in Christ should be to the praise of His glory. In Him you also *trusted*, after you heard the word of truth, the gospel of your salvation; in whom also, having believed, you were sealed with the Holy Spirit of promise, who is the guarantee of our inheritance until the redemption of the purchased possession, to the praise of His glory" (Eph. 1:3-13).

My fellow pilgrim traveler, Jesus is coming. Are you ready? If you had any inhibitions or reasons to withhold your Praises and Worship to God, I urge you to get rid of them now, for I know that when you are through reading this book, the zeal and knowledge of His will shall consummate you to the point of no return to the world of sin.

I reflect on what God said to Miriam and Aaron: "If there is a prophet among you, I will speak to him in dreams or send an Angel with the message to him, but my servant Moses, I speak with him face to face as a man speaks to his friend." Jesus said, "My sheep know my voice and a stranger's voice they will not follow."

My desires and prayers are to experience pervasively God's presence, while certainly knowing His voice, as Moses did and to further perceive and eradicate evil influences for the salvation of souls en route to the Kingdom of Heaven. And if you are not on the journey back to where you belong, you will, through this book of Hindsight *(perception after the fact)*, Insight *(a clear discernment)*, and Foresight *(looking forward or prudence)*, earnestly give attention.

Throughout the subsequent chapters, you will experience the revealed Word of Life and directions that undoubtedly will transform your life to please God, while guiding you back to Eternity. The scriptures do substantially appropriate what God reveals in these End Times to His Prophet for you, the Pilgrim traveling on the way to Glory.

ONE

The Perfect Praise

Our journey begins with the scriptures to validate genuine and true spiritual experiences, and to confirm the obvious differences of fallacies and truths. Moreover, the scriptures are the foundation of our Christian faith. And therefore, guards against errors and false doctrines. We must try the teachings and dogmas by the Word of God and search them diligently, for in them we think we have eternal life. Apostle Paul wrote, For when they should have been teachers, they had need to be taught again which *is* the first principles of the oracles of God. But strong meat belong to them that are of full age, *even* those who by reason of use have their senses exercised to discern both good and evil (Heb. 5:12-1).

"But as it is written, Eye hath not seen, nor ear heard, neither have entered into the heart of man, the things which God hath prepared for them that love him. But God hath revealed *them* unto us by his Spirit: for the Spirit searcheth all things, yea, the deep things of God.

Our God and Creator significantly put in order times and seasons to suite His divine will and purpose for the material world (Heb. 1:1-2; Eph. 2:7 and 3:5). He orchestrated His plan sequentially through time called dispensations.

There are nine dispensations, and we are at the seventh called Grace, which is greatest in length. The first is Dispensation of Angels. As the name portrays, angelic beings occupied this period—for how long (measuring by time) is not certain, but according to Genesis 1:1-2 and 3:1 and Job 38:4-7, the foundations were laid, suggesting a period before the beginning. The angels were on probation to prove obedience to God.

Does the Omnipotent God, who knows all things, proves or tests His children? Yes! He is just and true and would not force praise and worship to Himself on any being. Such must come forth of the immortal and mortal enthusiastically, i.e., *showing passionate interest with veneration, love, and devotion.* He gave self-governing will to establish His righteousness.

What glory would God receive from beings programmed just for one thing? Look at the heavenly story from the Bible; the most magnificent of all the heavenly beings failed the test and judgment was made on him and his followers. So things created and programed for just one purpose (or more) cannot give true adoration and glory. Much like empty-headed computers that can only do what is commanded or programed. Definitely have no feelings of pity, love, hate and sense of right and wrong. Take a look at God's description of the super being he created.

The Lord GOD Almighty spoke to Lucifer; Thou sealed up the sum, full of wisdom, and perfect in beauty. Thou hast been in Eden the garden of God; every precious stone *was* thy covering, the sardius, topaz, and the diamond, the beryl, the onyx, and the jasper, the sapphire, the emerald, and the carbuncle, and gold: the workmanship of thy tab rets and of thy pipes was prepared in thee in the day that thou was created. Thou *art* the anointed cherub that covered; and I have set thee *so*: thou were upon the holy mountain of God; thou hast walked up and down in the midst of the stones of fire.

"Thou *wast* perfect in thy ways from the day that thou was created, till iniquity was found in thee. By the multitude of thy merchandise they have filled the midst of thee with violence, and thou hast sinned: therefore I will cast thee as profane out of the mountain of God: and I will destroy thee, O covering cherub, from the midst of the stones of fire (holiness of God). Thine heart was lifted up because of thy beauty, thou hast corrupted thy wisdom by reason of thy brightness: I will cast thee to the ground, I will lay thee before kings, that they may behold thee" (Ezek. 28:11-17, KJV)

There were two Gardens of Eden: The first was Garden of God, where Lucifer and other angelic beings subsisted (*before Adam*). And there, sin originated among the angels and pre-Adamites.

King of Tyrus is an Epithet of Lucifer, the anointed Cherub (*one that covers*), who was created to give God perfect praise. Tyre *[tire]* (*rock*)—an ancient seaport city of the Phoenicians situated north of Israel. It was the principle seaport of the Phoenician coast, about 40 kilometers (25 miles) south of Sidon and 56 kilometers (*35 miles*) north of Carmel. It consisted of two cities: a rocky coastal city on the mainland and a small island city.

The island city was just off the shore. The mainland was on a coastal plain, a strip only 24 kilometers (*15 miles*) long and 3 kilometers (*2 miles*) wide. Behind the plain of Tyre stood the rocky mountains of Lebanon. Tyre was easily defended because it had the sea on the west, the mountains on the east, and several other rocky cliffs (*one famous "Ladder of Tyre"*) around it, making it difficult to invade.

Further explanation of the Creator's statement and into what is written about him is, "*Thou sealest* (to be the thing that ensures that something happens or that completes) *the sum* (the combined total amount or quantity of something) *of wisdom* (the ability to make sensible decisions and judgments based on personal knowledge and experience) *and perfect in beauty* (the combination of qualities that make something pleasing and impressive to look at, listen to, touch, smell, or taste)."

Did Lucifer put on those entire characteristics on his own, or was it genetic? Keep in mind that he was a created being. No, they were placed in him at time of his creation. "Thou hast been in Eden the garden of God; every precious stone *was* thy covering: the sardius, topaz, and the diamond; the beryl, the onyx, and the jasper; the sapphire, the emerald, and the carbuncle, and gold: the workmanship of thy tab rets and of thy pipes was *prepared in thee in the day that thou was created.*"

Ten precious stones are mentioned here for his covering (*i.e., his protection*). All were made of inflexible substance, making an impregnable jacket for protection.

God's promises are depicted here as "*every precious stone,*" telling us that we should desire spiritual gifts and cover ourselves to bring about divine protection from the onslaught of the enemy of souls. Keep in mind also that precious stones mentioned here do not lose their values, thus portraying that time and eternity cannot diminish the promises of God. And in every promise of God, are seeds for miracles.

The tambourine (*a shallow single-headed drum with jingling metallic disks in its frame, held in one hand and played by shaking it or striking it with the free hand*) and pipes (i.e., *trombone, saxophone, trumpet—all wind instruments*) were fashioned in him, making him the master musician.

His voice sounded as when a whole orchestra plays along with the drums (tambourine) to keep the beat. This remarkable being that walked up and down in the midst of the stones of fire (fire *typifies the Wrath of God*), covered the throne and gave *perfect praises* to God.

Wrath is the personal manifestation of God's holy, moral character in judgment against sin. His wrath is neither an impersonal process nor irrational and fitful like anger. It is in no way vindictive or malicious. God's anger directed holy indignation—against sin. God's wrath is an expression of His holy love. If God is not a God of wrath, His love is no more than frail, worthless sentimentality; the concept of mercy would then be meaningless, and the Cross was a cruel and unnecessary experience for His Son. M.H.C.

The Bible declares that all people are "by nature children of wrath" (Eph. 2:3) and that the wrath of God is disclosed from heaven against all ungodliness and unrighteousness of men, who quell the truth in unrighteousness. Since Christians have been vindicated by the blood of Jesus, we shall be saved from God's anger because of Him.

The enormousness of God's love was demonstrated in the Cross at Calvary where His only Son felt pronounced fury for our sake.

The wrath of God did not denounce and put away Satan while he was a perfect being, for he did everything he was created to do. Whenever he was in the midst of the stones of fire, his beauty attracted praises to God from the Holy Angels. God receives praises from true hearts only. As they praised God, Lucifer's jacket glowed and Holy beams radiated, transforming him to be the Bright and Morning Star that takes to mean, "Son of the Morning." He was in charge of protecting the Throne and leading praise and worship.

He is seen as the brilliance of the fundamental nature of God (*the quality or nature that identifies or makes it what it is*).

Gifts bequeathed, are to uphold worship and praise to the only wise God and not for self-glorification. Ah! But he coveted the very thing that he was created to guard. His heart was lifted in self-worth but could only lead to destruction. Pride precedes destruction, and an overconfident spirit before collapse.

Did God not know that Lucifer would have fallen? Yes; then why did he create him thus? The answer is that the omniscient God placed him on probation, just as he did humankind. You must understand that heavenly and earthly beings have a sovereign personal will and do boast command of their own lives. However, God has set *boundaries for life and death*, which gives the opportunity to choose. Hence, for this cause or reason, probation is enforced.

Satan miserably failed the test and was immediately malformed from Son of the Morning to Prince of Darkness. Beings that do not have a sovereign will are incapable of making choices, for they live by instinct, i.e., a powerful impulse that feels natural rather than reasoned (*such as animals*).

The profound truth is, "Eternity has no end, and so the good or the bad actions could go on and keep on going while existing at hand. God so created time to hold keys for maturity toward bringing about ends, to punish evil, and for development of humanity and promote direction to perfection for life with God. No need to fear, for the enemy is defeated. Jesus was a witness, and His report we believe. He said, "I beheld the earth, and, lo, *it was* without form, and void; and the heavens, and they *had* no light. I beheld the mountains, and, lo, they trembled, and all the hills moved lightly. I beheld, and, lo, *there was* no man, and all the birds of the heavens were fled. I beheld, and, lo, the fruitful place *was* a wilderness, and all the cities thereof were broken down at the presence of the LORD, *and* by his fierce anger" (Jer. 4:23-26).

He made Lucifer to foster *the Perfect Praise* for His pleasure. Such the like, You are worthy, O Lord, to receive glory and honor and power: for you have created all things, and for your pleasure, they are and were created, amen.

"Thou, *even* thou, *art* LORD alone; thou hast made heaven, the heaven of heavens, with their entire host, the earth, and all *things* that *are* therein, the seas, and all that *is* therein, and thou preserves them all; and the host of heaven worships thee."

The second, named Adam's Garden of Eden where sin originated with the Adamites (Gen. 2:8; 3:24). Both were destroyed of the same cause: Sin. Genesis records the recreation of the earth or the beginning of time. *God did not formulate time, for that which is (be) and/or what exists eternally.* The heavenly hosts are eternal, and time indicates a period that has an end.

God further turns His attention to the man He formed and fashioned from the earth made of lower substance (*a type of birth*). Adam was archetype *(prototype)* on probation, and that is why he failed.

Nevertheless, events occurred just as the Creator planned it. Adam briefly experienced time without end.

We now arrive at the second era called Dispensation of Innocence (Gen. 2:8-15, 25; 3:7). The number of days that innocence lasted was just about six. Man failed (Gen. 3:1-24; Rom. 3:23 and 5:12-21), and God pronounced the curse (Gen. 3:14-19; 23-24; Rom. 16:20), but alongside sentence, there is emancipation. God promised a Redeemer (Gen. 3:15-21 and 4:1-7; Mat. 1:21 and 26:28; Eph. 1:7) named Jesus, meaning Savior.

"The time past without dates is an introduction (Pr. 8:22; John. 1:1; Acts 15-18; Heb. 1:10) to the whole Bible and all history, for it marks the boundary between time and eternity. It is not a summarized statement of what is to follow, for it mentions Heaven first, while the following verses mention the *earth* first. Job 38:4-7 makes it clear that the heavens were created first; else, the stars could not have rejoiced when the earth was created." The Son is the Word alive from the Father that has his own ability to create things exactly as intended.

Before we enter the events of time and the material world, journey with me into Eternity to uncover the segment of Satan's origin, not Lucifer's, for the Bible revealed his origin in Ezekiel 28, explained earlier.

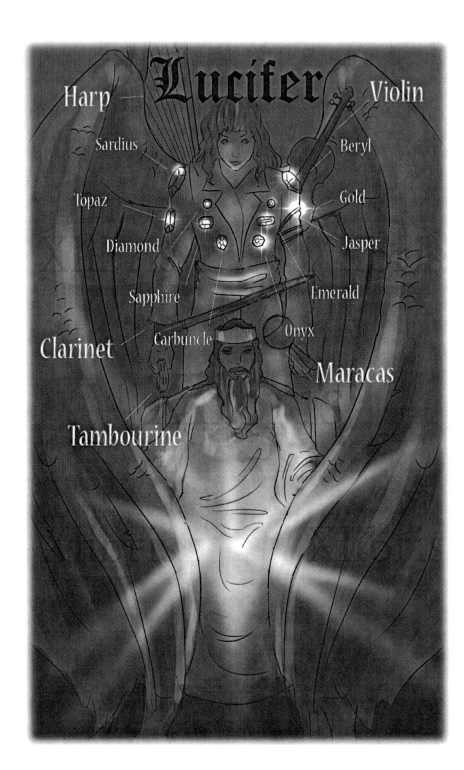

Two

Satan's Beginning

God created Lucifer and the Angelic beings.

Colossians 1:12-20 states, "Giving thanks unto the Father, who made us meet to be partakers of the inheritance of the saints in light; who delivered us out of the power of darkness, and translated us into the kingdom of the Son of his love; in whom we have our redemption, the forgiveness of our sins: who is the image of the invisible God, the firstborn of all creation; for in him were all things created, in the heavens and upon the earth, things visible and things invisible, whether thrones or dominions or principalities or powers; all things have been created through him, and unto him; and he is before all things, and in him all things consist.

In the prophet Isaiah's statement of him, the word "perfect" is used, and it means, conforming absolutely to the description or definition of the ideal type. Let us observe that all of God's creation, whether of heavenly or earthly realm, are perfect. He cannot make mistakes.

At the onset of creation, only God had knowledge of good and evil. Knowledge and experience go hand in hand, but you can argue that if God has knowledge of sin, then He partook of it. Not so—He is not subject to the same laws as created beings. "Let no one say when he is tempted, I am tempted by God: for God cannot be tempted by evil, nor does He Himself tempt anyone. However, each one is tempted when he is drawn away by his own desires and enticed. Then, when desire has conceived, it gives birth to sin; and sin, when it is full-grown, brings forth death" (James 1:13-15).

We must acknowledge that prior to Lucifer's insurgence, no heavenly created beings knew (nor partook) of sin. Sin was never in Heaven and still cannot enter, even after the infiltration none remained, for the coals of fire situated at the front of the throne that Lucifer danced in, burned profusely preserving God's nature. Fir is a purifying agent. Satan and all the fallen angels are barred forever from God's presence. Only the redeemed born-again children of the Spirit and the blood of Jesus Christ can enter.

However, the question is, "Why did Satan sin?" He was made with exceptional beauty, the masterpiece of the heavenly beings; furthermore, there was none created like him.

Before I give the answer, a foundation or basis of truth must be set. So let us explore governing laws.

The basic collective idea is that everything can be explained by one thing—matter. Matter is the total explanation for space, nature, man, psychic consciousness, human intelligence, and every other aspect of existence. Collectivism then assigns the task of knowing all truth to science.

If science can get to know everything about matter, then it can get to know about everything. Conclusively, matter is accepted as the beginning and ending of all reality. Taking the concept of matter, collectivism then sets forth to answer three questions: What is the origin of energy or motion in nature? What causes galaxies, solar system, planets, animals, and all kingdoms of nature to increase their numerical quantity constantly? What are the origin of life, the origin of species, and the origin of consciousness and mind? Marx and Engels answer all these questions with three laws: the law of opposites, the law of negation, and the law of transformation.

Constant measurable growth by a certain group often results in a "significant increase" in a specific characteristic whereby a completely new form or person is produced. This theory draws many parallels to the Theory of Evolution. Some philosophers concluded that matter is not only auto-dynamic and inclined to increase itself numerically, but through quantitative accumulations, it is also inherently capable of "springing" to new forms. So What is life?

Let us explore the truth about Good and Evil. We read that God is good and that He is love. Before human beings were created, the Creator brought light into being: "Then God said, Let there be (physical) light; and there was light. And God saw the light, that it *was good*" (Gen. 1:3-4). *Light*—illumination, the opposite of darkness.

The Bible also speaks of light as the symbol of God's presence and righteous activity. Light has been associated with the presence, truth, and redemptive activity of God since creation.

Throughout the Bible, light represents truth, goodness, and God's redemptive work. So since God is the ruler of light with all that is good, then Evil, which is the opposite of good, is the law of darkness.

Darkness is the absence of light. Darkness existed before the light of creation. Since darkness was associated with the chaos that existed before the creation of the material world, it came to be associated with everything that's evil, bad luck, or affliction (Job 17:12; 21:17). Darkness was also equated with death. In Sheol, the land of the dead, there is only darkness. Darkness also symbolizes human ignorance of God's will and, thus, is associated with sin (Job 24:13-17).

Darkness also describes the condition of those who have not yet seen the light concerning Jesus, and those who deliberately turn away from that light (John 3:19-20). Hating the light will bring condemnation (Col. 1:13; 2 Pet. 2:17). Living in extreme darkness describes those who, at the end of time, have not repented. "And the fifth angel poured out his vial upon the seat of the beast, and his kingdom was full of darkness; and they gnawed their tongues for pain" (Rev. 16:10). "This then is the message which we have heard of him, and declare unto you, that God is light, and in him is no darkness at all. If we say that we have fellowship with him, and walk in darkness, we lie, and do not the truth: But if we walk in the light, as he is in the light, we have fellowship one with another, and the blood of Jesus Christ his Son cleanses us from all sin" (1 John 1:5-7).

In the parable of the talents, the master says to the man who hid his one talent in the ground, "Cast ye the unprofitable servant into outer darkness: there shall be weeping and gnashing of teeth" (Matt. 25:30). To unfaithful Israel, Jesus said, "But the children of the kingdom shall be cast out into outer darkness: there shall be weeping and gnashing of teeth" (Matt. 8:12). Darkness, on the other hand, symbolizes error, evil, and the works of Satan.

Several of the miracles recorded in the Bible are related to light and darkness: the "Pillar of Fire" that guided the Israelites in the wilderness (Exod. 3:21), the sun standing still at Gibeon at Joshua's request (Josh. 10:12-13), and the fall of darkness at midday when Jesus was being crucified (Matt. 27:45). Misguided fascination with light caused some cultures of the ancient world to worship the sun and moon. Ur in Babylonia and several of the Canaanite cities had elaborate systems of moon worship.

Use of light was common in the festivals of the Greek cults, especially those honoring Dionysus and Apollo.

Satan's beginning continues: Again, I say that Lucifer did not transform himself to be Satan. He is a created being; he had help from the dark side. However, all created beings, whether heavenly or earthly, spirit or material, were created for the glory of God and have the power of choice. His heart was open to pride (a high inordinate opinion of one's own dignity, importance, merit, or superiority, whether as cherished in the mind or displayed in bearing, conduct etc.) and gave place and access to darkness. Darkness of evil could not overcome to wipe out the light of God, but they coexist, for it is the absence of light, and it vehemently works to destroy all that is good. Because it cannot exist in light, it sought a being capable of handling its gruesome power, and for this reason, Lucifer was chosen and changed from Morning Star or Anointed Cherub to Prince of Darkness (not a king as the absolute ruler), and he died to the Light.

This death takes to mean eternal darkness, a separation from the God of lights where everything is good. It is the domain or region of absolute horror and essence of the true temperament that make evil what it is. No spiritual or earthly being can undergo its infliction of violent punishment and exist. For this reason, God reserves bodies for those who will enter because of disobedience and rejection of Jesus Christ, our Savior. This realm is feared by all heavenly and earthly beings. In this book, the chapter "What in Hell Do You Want", gives further insight to this place and the condition while in eternal death.

Lucifer boasted titles of "Son of the Morning," "Anointed Cherub," and "One who protects" and danced in the coal of fire that was set before the throne of Almighty God, his creator. The extreme value placed self-worth (known as pride) was determined above his Creator, put his light out, the very essence and purpose of his existence, thus making him a fallen star forever into blackness. "And he (Jesus)said unto them, I beheld Satan as lightning fall from heaven" (Luke 10:18). Let us be somber and of a humble and modest disposition, for with position comes great responsibilities and a tremendous opportunity to fail.

The law of opposite took effect as Evil aggressively ceased possession of his being. Consequently, darkness entered the realm and presence of light but only by way of that created being whose heart was lifted high in him to covet and reject the love and goodness of his God.

Bear in mind that the carrier or vessel of darkness cannot remain in the light, for the works thereof are evil and will contaminate the whole. Evil seeks to dominate to destruction, for such is its nature. Be forewarned to keep your heart with assiduousness for out of it flows the substance of living.

During the Exodus or wilderness wonderings, the people who knew God and saw his mighty acts upon the Egyptians, did not glorify him as God. Instead they were unthankful with futile ingenuities that gave way to darkness.

Openly claimed to be wise, they became empty headed, sadly resulting in converting the magnificence of the everlasting God into images of weak-willed man, birds, four-footed beasts, and slithering things. So the creator God handed them over to sinfulness through their own yearning hearts, to disgrace between themselves. But they miserably changed the truth of God into a lie, and revered and served the beast more than the Creator, blessed be His name for ever.

Let this serve as a reminder to mankind that God is to serve and worship, and not one's self. Solomon wrote in Ecclesiastes, Chapter 12, to remember our Creator in the days our youth, concluding that the whole duty of man is to fear God and keep His commandments.

God and His Word (the Bible) are frequently represented as lights or lamps to enlighten and guide the believer (1 John 1:5). "Your word is a lamp to my feet and a light to my path" (Ps. 119:105).

The Psalmist also declared, "The Lord is my light and my salvation; whom shall I fear?" (Ps. 27:1). Light is also used as a symbol of holiness and purity. Paul counseled the Christians at Rome to "put on the armor of light" (Rom. 13:12).

The New Testament presents Jesus as the personification of light or divine illumination: "I am the light of the world" (John 8:12). Jesus plainly stated that those who rejected this divine light would bring judgment upon themselves (John 3:19-21). Jesus and the New Testament writers extended the figure of light to include faithful Christian witnesses, who were called "children of light" (Eph. 5:8). "This then is the message which we have heard of him, and declare unto you, that God is light, and in him is no darkness at all" (1 John 1:5). Since God is light, Darkness is evil.

If Marxist theory is accurate, then we can accept the fact that God is light, and evil is an opponent stemmed from darkness. And on the other hand, Lucifer now Satan or adversary, is controlled thereby. He was a cherubim and maestro in charge of the praise team in Heaven to order Praise Glory and Honor to the King of kings, the Ruler of the universe; he knew what it meant. It was on that basis that he envied his Creator God. We read, "For thou hast said in thine heart, I will ascend into heaven, I will exalt my throne above the stars (angelic beings that hold ranks) of God: I will sit also upon the mount of the congregation, in the sides of the north: I will ascend above the heights of the clouds; I will be like the most High, how art thou fallen from heaven, O Lucifer, son of the morning! *How* art thou cut down to the ground, which didst weaken the nations! (Isa. 14:12).

Five times the Devil said, *I will,* showing that *five times* his determination to achieve absolute glory and praise, but he was defeated. Five is the number of Angels. Alas, his pending doom was pronounced.

Satan, the covetous one, could not appreciate the fact that God gave this lower creature (man) the glorious position as *Ruler of the works of His hands*. The question was asked, "*What is man,* that You should magnify him, that You should set Your heart on him?"

Man made of perishable material and of substance lower than the angels, has dominion over the works of God's hands. Lord, *what is mankind,* that you take knowledge of. *What is man* that You are mindful of him or the son of man that You take care of him? (Heb. 2:6).

The fact that God breathed His breath into man and he became a living soul bewildered and distressed the Devil; moreover, then, he yearned for replication, for that masterpiece (man, the crown of creation) holds that which is most desirable to him, and if he had control over him, he would get glory. As was the spirit of God in man, so the Devil desired to enter in. The body of man is the temple of God, and evil and good cannot live in it as light and darkness cannot occupy the same space. For the Devil to have total control of any human being, that individual must be totally null and void of God and His knowledge.

Furthermore, the body was not made to house evil, which is why when one is possessed of demons, there is disfigurement, alterations to the corporeal, and emotional make up; the body must die of exasperation. "The wages of sin is death, but the gift of God is eternal life" (Rom. 6:23). To sin means to miss the mark for life and true spiritual union with our Creator.

And still Satan constantly hounded for a means to sever God's relationship with man because he thought that he deserved all the glory, honor, and praise that belong to God. He found the woman as the means. Curious always, not knowing everything, she was forced to notice the tree and wondered, but she knew the command of God, for Adam had told her. However, her inquisitiveness got the best of her.

It opened the door of opportunity for the Devil to go in and sow his seed of doubt which led to the death of man, the friend of God; His masterpiece was now broken, and his glory had been taken away.

Here Satan accused God of hiding the truth: "And the woman said unto the serpent, 'We may eat of the fruit of the trees of the garden: But of the fruit of the tree which *is* in the midst of the garden, God hath said, Ye shall not eat of it, neither shall ye touch it, lest ye die.' And the serpent said unto the woman, 'Ye shall not surely die: *For God doth know* that in the day ye eat thereof, then your eyes shall be opened, and ye shall be as gods, knowing good and evil.'

"And when the woman saw that the tree *was good for food*, and that it *was* pleasant to the eyes, and a tree to be desired to *make one wise*, she took of the fruit thereof, and did eat, and gave also unto her husband with her; and he did eat." He stimulated Eve's curiosity from which he invoked the *need to know*, with the sad result of doubting God their Creator and friend, thus bringing a propos for man's reason to fail. She passed on *the seed of death* (the seed is sin) to her husband, and he did eat.

The Bible records that we were once in Him, as a seed is in the loins of a father. God did not ban man to perish, but He made a way for him to go again to the life of a son, as the wasteful son returned to his home, in the book of Luke. You must understand that we came from God who sits high, and His ways are higher than our ways.

Right in the beginning, we see the original intention of the Father. He made man in His image and in His likeness with all abilities but only in a lesser degree and with a sovereign will. He never projected man to be a servant doing menial jobs; but a son, for the son is an absolute manifestation of his father, thus making Adam one and the same in power of the works of God's hands. He is the ultimate chef-d'oeuvre, the pinnacle, and glee of design, and God went to Eden in the cool of the day, to commune with him.

What they talked and laughed about is unknown, but it was enough to get the Devil green-eyed. God caused the first man (*Adam, a type of Christ*) to fall in a deep sleep *(a kin to death)* while giving life to the first woman, Eve (*a type of the Church*). Here Satan got angrier, for man hereby was granted the power to procreate but he (*Satan*) could not.

Remember the Bible records that the only thing Satan could produce was, and still is, LIES, making him the father of it. Just imagine what the world would be if Satan could father other beings like himself. We have more than we can handle with one of him, but thanks be to our omniscient God, who so ordained time and purpose for everything. Satan, on the other hand, has claimed without permission many souls as his own but only because their lusts and sins gave him that power.

Jesus told some Jews that they were children of the Devil and everything he does is of his own.

Three

The fall of Adam

The Serpent (*another title of Satan*) did not know that good and evil could not occupy the same space and that for him to boast power over any man, the man must completely be unfounded (*without foundation*) and void of God and His knowledge (*light to the soul*). Still, if it were that, if that man was seized upon by the Devil while he is in cognition (*ability to acquire knowledge, awareness*), the dread of darkness (*evil is densely dark*) would cause the physical part of him to deteriorate. The body was not made a house for evil; it would most absurdly be disfigured and perish, definitely not a thing of beauty.

Evil cannot maintain beauty, only good can. Which is why the word says, Shall not I the take the members of Christ, (body) and make *them* the members of a harlot, God forbid.

God prearranged everything for His own purpose. Adam was unique and distinct from the animals in several ways. His formation is described independently from that of the animals and the rest of God's innovative acts (Gen. 1:3-25; 1:26-27; 2:7). God breathed into Adam's body of dust the divine breath of life, and man became a living being (Gen. 2:7). He also made him in His own image and likeness.

The exact words are, "Let Us make man, in our image, according to Our likeness" (Gen. 1:26). Apostle Paul interprets this to mean that God created man with spiritual, rational, emotional, and moral qualities (Eph. 4:24-32; Col. 3:8-10). He was a type of Christ but made to fall short so that Jesus the only begotten Son of God (*the second Adam*) could come into view.

Now this I say, brethren, that flesh and blood cannot inherit the kingdom of God; neither doth corruption inherit incorruption. There is a natural body, and there is a spiritual body. And so it is written, the first man Adam was made a living soul; and could only produce earthly things.

The last Adam *was made* a quickening (alive) spirit; Howbeit that *was* not first which is spiritual, but that which is natural; and afterward that which is spiritual.

The first man is of the earth, earthly: the second man is the Lord from heaven. As is the earthly, such are they also that are earthly: and as is the heavenly, such are they also that are heavenly. And as we have borne the image of the earthy, we shall also bear the image of the heavenly. The second man from heaven produces heavenly and eternal things. Here we know that God made man to inherit the Kingdom of Heaven. The divine order of man is, first earthly and then transforms to be heavenly, through death. The first son had precedence over the other sons of the family.

Adam was known to be the lower (earthly), from which could not rule according to God's Holy Will, consequently, the fall. As soon as man fell, God gave a promise of atonement, and we have a divine assurance that Satan, the cause and perpetuator of the curse, would be defeated by the "seed of a woman" (*a term for the Incarnate Son of God*).

We know that a woman does not produce seeds; it comes only from a man, but God intended to bewilder the wise and prudent (the serpent) by means of using the base (man) things of the earth. Therefore, He caused the woman to produce a seed that would redeem humanity from the curse of the law.

Remember this that Spirit cannot atone for flesh nor can flesh for spirit, for this reason came the incarnation of Jesus Christ. Subsequently, God made man lower than the angels and placed him in time, where he can learn faith (*a quality Satan does not have*) in order to be like his Creator and live with Him.

The way was set forth from the Garden of Eden at the moment God said, "The woman's seed shall bruise thy head and I will put enmity between you and the woman, and between your seed and her Seed; *He shall bruise your head*, and you shall bruise His heel" (Gen. 3:15). The bruising of Jesus's heel was His death on the Cross by which He accomplished our redemption. In the New Testament, the path is personified as Christ. He declared, "*I am the way*, the truth and the life, no man cometh to the Father but by me."

Four

The Curse

By instigation of the Devil, the seed of sin sown in the woman brought about disobedience, when she doubted God's command. The sad result was death. She was able to pass that seed onto her husband, by way of gaining his trust, thus, in due course, corrupting the world. Please note that the same moment that Adam believed the Devil's lie (i.e., *saying he was not created in the image of God*), he fell. He was tricked into receiving that lie, accordingly giving up the position he held. The mortal man made in God's image inescapably operated as a direct reflection, a mirror image of his Maker. Alas! Now to exist as a mere creature of lower substance, subjected to die.

Alas, the earnings of sin are death but the gift of God is eternal life, through Jesus Christ our Lord. Unknowingly, they chose death. God, however, had a plan to bring life back to humanity through death. Now let us look at what was said here.

"And the LORD God said unto the serpent, Because thou hast done this, thou *art* cursed above all cattle, and above every beast of the field; upon thy belly shalt thou go, and dust shalt thou eat all the days of thy life."

Isaiah 14 records the iniquity that was found in Satan's heart: For thou hast said in your heart, I will ascend into heaven, I will exalt my throne above the stars of God: I will sit also upon the mount of the congregation, in the sides of the north: I will ascend above the heights of the clouds; I will be like the most High.

Yet thou shalt be brought down to hell, to the sides of the pit.

That ambition cultivated iniquity in the serpent's heart and ultimately reduced him to be the most appalling of all beasts—to crawl on its belly, signifying the low nature and punishment of a malevolent mind; to eat dust along with his food and be transformed to an antagonizing creature; along with a nature to strike at man's heel but only to have his head bruised or crushed, an enemy forever.

The serpent was subtle more (*slight, clever, witty*) than any beast. It had the power of speech and sauntered upright, half on its tail. It was a wonder to look at. Eve was amazed at its stance and knew that it was older and truly more knowledgeable than she was (*moreover, he was the master of persuasions*). All the same, her curiosity got the best of her. "And he said unto the woman, Yes did truly God said, you shall not eat of every tree of the garden?

"And the woman said unto the serpent, We may eat of the fruit of the trees of the garden: But of the fruit of the tree which *is* in the midst of the garden, God hath said, we shall not eat of it, neither shall ye touch it, or we die. And the serpent said unto the woman, You shall not surely die: For God does know that in the day you eat of it, your eyes shall be opened, and you shall be as gods, knowing good and evil. And when the woman saw that the tree *was* good for food, and that it *was* pleasant to the eyes, and a tree to be desired to make *her* wise, she eat of the fruit, and gave also unto her husband with her; and he did eat."

Let's look at the points made here by the Devil: (1) *You shall not surely die*: accuses God of lying. (2) *God knows that*: accuses God of hiding the truth and that God doesn't want anyone to be His equal, that it was really placed in the Garden for them to have. (3) *The day you eat*: time is set for opportunities and possibilities. (4) *Your eyes shall be opened*: instant change. (5) *You shall be as gods*: promises and hope. (6) *Know good and evil*: wisdom and power.

He craved all those virtues but only to his demise. The serpent did not tell her of man's composition, for God had said that He would make man in His own image and likeness, thus creating him to be like Him. A son is like his father. The Jews crucified Jesus because He said He is the Son of God, making Him equal with God. Adam was created a Son of God but did not apprehend or realize this truth.

Today, many of God's dear children are deprived of their inheritance in the same manner, for this reason, the motivation to know God's will for their lives. Regrettably, through his swaying words, he tempted her, and she conceded.

So, He drove out the man; and he placed at the east of the Garden of Eden, Cherubim and a flaming sword which turned every way, *to keep the way* of the tree of life."

Now, *the earth had the essence of life from God* and could only produce good things, for God saw that it was good. There was nothing to hurt, nothing feral and chaotic, but all was peace and harmony.

Next is the Dispensation of Conscience (Gen. 2:15-17, 25; 3:1-6, 10). Length of time spanned about 1656 years. The promise of redemption is carried on through Adam's seed while retaining the knowledge of punishment and the rewards of obedience. As human beings, they were to do well with the internal voice called conscience (sense of right and wrong).

Adam's descendants failed, judgment pronounced, but alongside the verdict was redemption, by way of the Angel that went before to show them the way and reveal the will of God (*a type of the Holy Spirit*) (Gen. 6:18; 7:1-3; 8:20-22).

Adam was made sinless (a living soul) with a godly nature, but the moment he accepted the forbidden fruit (good and evil), another nature was fashioned in him and brought about death, consequently initiating corruption in the whole of creation.

"For since by man came death, by man came also the resurrection of the dead. For as in Adam all die, even so in Christ shall all be made alive. *But now is Christ risen from the dead, and become the first fruits of them that slept.*" This explains that the connection with God and mortal man severed, ultimately ensuing physical death. The choice was his, for He had hope and a promise (i.e., *back to Eternity*). However, God permitted life to continue, and in order for him to return to fellowship and union his Origin, a most worthy and acceptable mortal life must be *freely given, not taken*. Worthy means innocent, never partook of sin. It is a horrendous crime to take an innocent life and pronounces hatred of the Creator.

Now, there are two deaths: the Physical death and then the Spiritual. The Physical death occurs when the body ceases to function but the soul goes to God (Eccles. 12:7). The second death denotes eternal separation from God; this happens when God rejects the soul (*happens at the judgment seat of Christ*) and throws it in the eternal abyss.

Further studies suggest that *spirit cannot atone for flesh*. The question is, "Was there any flesh worthy to make atonement?" The answer is No. There was none, and for this reason, God ordained the incarnation of Christ, that is, He put on physical body (flesh) and of death (*remember, in Adam all die!*). In Christ, all are alive, and who could go and redeem Adam's fallen race? Only the Lamb of God was found worthy. Man's redemption was not contemptible; however, the price was incalculable.

I believe that God bankrupt Heaven to bring about man's salvation." For God so loved the world that He gave His only begotten Son, that whosoever believeth on should not perish but have eternal life. You see, God's ways are higher than our ways and so He couldn't accept fallen man to redeem himself, but still, only a man could. The omniscient God who designed all things, so allowed the fall in order to bring about the defeat of Satan and his works while appropriating redemption. Satan will pay the penalty for all that he has done, for sin does not go unpunished.

The God of love and mercy did not exact judgment or wretchedness on them (*Adam and Eve*) although He was angry, but His generosity is endless. He placed cherubim with flaming swords to keep the way to the tree of life, for mankind would corrupt it and unwittingly debar himself and his generations forever, with no hope of reconciliation. Nevertheless, God's plan for man's return was settled for he placed Angels with the flaming sword to keep the way to the tree of life, keeping it for those who have rinsed their robes and made them white in the blood of the Lamb. The way to the tree of life will be free for all born-again children of God. Nevertheless, for now, Adam and his generations must work the earth in order to eat bread for it is cursed, as is he. He must work hard to survive until death, when he goes back, dust-to-dust ashes to ashes.

In the Dispensation of Human Government that spanned about 427 years, man was given God's law with human government to rule faithfully, punish criminals, and to perfect praise, with worship.

Noah, the accepted man of faith, and his sons found grace in the eyes of God, but all others failed (Gen. 9:7). God confused their language, divided the earth, scattered them thither, and provided redemption through sacrificial offerings (sacrifices portray Christ's crucifixion for the sins of the world). At this instant, the path ordained for man to take on his return back to God is, to a certain extent, clearer (Gen. 8:20 and 12:8; Gal. 3:8; Heb. 3).

Five

From Death Came Life

The earth was created to produce good things freely, but Adam's curse covered all of creation. The earth is to be subdued and tilled because it will be unwilling to produce, yet it had the power to make man's lifespan possible. You see, he could not inherit paradise as a sinner.

Lifestyle before the fall was without unfavorable conditions, such as storms, thunders, or lightning, neither anything brutal nor meat eaters, nothing hurting or causing any hurt. God caused a mist to come up out of the ground and watered the plants. They truly lived in paradise until the moment of sin, everything changed.

Death is designed to destroy God's purpose for creation (life); nevertheless, Satan did not know that God would use the same destroyer to bring life. For this reason, we have the death of Jesus on the cross (*the second Adam, a quickening spirit*).

"And as Moses lifted up the serpent in the wilderness, even so must the Son of man be lifted up; For God so loved the world that he gave his only begotten Son that whosoever believeth in Him should not perish, but have eternal life. For God sent not his Son into the world to condemn the world but that the world through him might be saved" (John 3:16-17).

The serpent on the pole signifies the Crucifixion of Christ on which all who believe shall be saved from eternal death (*separation from God the Father of life without a hope*). Therefore, *the instrument of death became the object of life*, and *from death came life*.

The spirit alone is the promise and not just a given assurance. Jesus is the begotten Son of the Father and the first begotten of the dead. It's seen here that death gave birth to life. However, death is an enemy that will be trampled by Jesus, our conquering Savior. Thus, the scripture declares, "Death is swallowed up in victory; O! Death, where is thy sting; O! Grave, where is thy victory."

It is a decisive element to our quest for redemption, i.e., the fear of death (*eternal separation from God*). "The book of Revelation tells us that the fearful and unbelieving were cast into the lake of fire with the devil and his angels." Therefore, the Father of lights (*understanding and wisdom*) had to free humanity for them to compete for the prize of eternal life. Paul said in Ephesians, "I press toward the mark for the prize of the high calling in Christ Jesus."

What is that calling? Is it not life and to be joint heirs with Christ? In the Old Testament of types and shadows, we find that Sarah's womb was as good as dead. In the book of Genesis, Chapter 18, we read, "Abraham and Sarah *were* old *and* well stricken in age and barren; *and* it ceased to be with Sarah after the manner of women."

"Therefore Sarah laughed within herself, saying, after I am waxed old shall I have pleasure, my lord being old also? And the LORD said unto Abraham, Wherefore did Sarah laugh, saying, Shall I of a surety bear a child, which am old? Is anything too hard for the LORD? (Gen. 18:12-14).

Sarah was sterile and well-stricken in age; she had neither more monthly cycles, nor any chance of her ever giving birth, but however, that was God's way of preserving man's redemption. It was, by way, His promise and not by human strength or abilities.

Abraham lived in the Dispensation of Promise that spanned 430 years, starting from his call to the Exodus from Egypt (Gen. 12:1—Exod. 12:37). He was known as the father of faith, and he pleased God. It had an encouraging launch with true worship: life of faith, eternal future, Resurrection (from death came life), and prayer.

Because of his walk with God, all the families of the earth to this day are blessed (Gen. 17:1-22). His legacy was handed down to his sons, but they failed (Gen. 21:1-35; 25:24-49).

Sentence was well defined, and restoration was sited alongside, but not without much sacrifices and validations of God's Omnipotence (Exod. 12:20-30; 14:30-31). Here we see a type of Christ's shed blood and triumph over death, hell and the grave, while bringing His chosen people to the promise land (*a type of the heavenly city*). Soon afterwards the dispensation of Law took effect and spanned to the present age, about seventeen hundred and eighteen years (Gen. 8:15-Rev. 19:10); from the Exodus to the preaching of John the Baptist (Exod. 12:38-Mat. 2:23). They were to conform to approximately two thousand demands, rulings and orders of God. The Law provided guidance, stability, healing, protection and wealth, and was given through Judges, Prophets and Kings. But the leaders and the people fell short.

Six

Pathway: Back to God and to Eden

At this point of time, the man Abraham did not have power to give life, for he was old, but God repeatedly told them that His promises are true and that He would visit them (*in nine months*). The promise was to Abraham and Sarah, so the child Isaac was the son of promise, typifying the only begotten Son of God, the promised seed that would bruise Satan's head. Remember this: Sarah had no more eggs to produce, her womb was dried up, and, furthermore, she was barren. Therefore, God had to work a miracle on her, and old Abe.

This child was not of their own strength; it was a mystery of the spirit supernaturally fertilizing and strengthening their flesh to carry out the promise of the Father. Just as He spoke the word only and the world was created, it was not a difficult thing for God to do it again. The next time, it would be of a higher order where *the spirit alone is the promise,* unlike *the promise given* and carried out through the efforts of the man Abraham.

Redemption could only come by the spoken word of God. We read in the New Testament, "The Word became flesh and dwelled among men, and we beheld His glory as of the only begotten Son of the Father." *But is the curse a map that leads back to Eden, or a blessing in disguise?*

The path back to God and Eden was here pronounced by means of the seed (Jesus) of the woman, a judgment that would inflame the ultimate defeat of the Devil. The woman conceived and bore a seed of sin; she became the mother of all living and, consequently, was named Eve. To sin is to *forfeit rights* for fellowship with God for all *eternity*.

He is driven out of paradise, out of the presence of his Creator, to ascertain perfection. He lost Glory; because of sin now, he is confused and led astray by the enemy but must find his way back to fellowship and communion with his maker. The course that is set before him interprets as a "manner of lifestyle" (i.e., *devotion and faith*) to which he is bound to apprehend in order to regain his title, "Keeper of the Works of God's Hands."

Nevertheless, God put a "Light" called Hope, a homing beacon (*an idiom*) in Adam, at the time of the enunciation of the curse, to impress on him to return one day; but until then, he was given time to acquire knowledge, nurture faith, trust, and redemption in order to stand in the presence of God throughout eternity.

This principle is written in man's genes and carried on throughout generations. God does not hold one man or a nation responsible, but all as one. If left imprudent or rash, time and the evil one could wipe it (*the principle*) out. However, our Creator God will not leave humankind alone, for where there is no order, there is chaos.

For God said, I will never leave thee, nor forsake thee. So that we may boldly say, The Lord *is* my helper, and I will not fear what man shall do unto me. He will be there to assist in rehabilitating the crown of His creation. Our Father and Creator made man to give Him glory; that is why the Psalmist said, "You crowned him with your glory and gave him dominion over the works of your fingers."

He was able to experience sentiments through humanity (*the flesh*). I am not saying that God does not have feelings, for He formulated such in our nature. To explain what this means

Jehovah Adonai restricted his own powers in order to comply to his own design for free proper managers of righteousness. Such act does not make him less omnipotent (all-powerful). It makes it viable; and aids in molding the independent will of man.

Here it's seen that God does not structure the will, choices and acts of man, but holds him accountable should he act contrary to the best of the good of posterity.

We further reflect on the moment before the destruction of the cities of Sodom and Gomorrah (Gen. 18:20-22): "And the LORD said, because the cry of Sodom and Gomorrah is great, and because their sin is very grievous; I will go down now, and see whether they have done altogether according to the cry of it, which is come unto me; and if not, I will know. And the men turned their faces from thence, and went toward Sodom: but Abraham stood yet before the LORD."

God's love compelled Him to go to those cities and a have first-hand familiarity of the cry of the sins of the inhabitants; their cries went up to

Him (as the blood of Abel). Did He need to do it? No, He is God and can do what pleases Him. The Father, who is a consuming fire, is such a just and righteous God that He would not destroy a people until He had first-hand experience of their circumstances. In attendance, He could better judge them, for there is a great distance between man and God and between the Heaven and the earth.

Today, the Holy Spirit proceeds from both the Father and his Son Christ Jesus, dwells in us.

Seven

The Keeper

There is always the need to know, but curiosity was not a part of man's construction, because God made him innocent (sinless) with all suitability, and boasted all knowledge that was essential to live in the presence of the Almighty. The Devil knew that they were dependent, and were created a little lower than the angels: conditionally made, limited to time and space, crowned with God's glory, completely loyal and obedient to his Creator until the need to know was spawned into their spirits by the Devil.

Why did our Creator God give man the occupation of *Ruler of the works of His hands?* In addition, what was he to keep? There were no wild animals nor rough bushes; everything grew to its proper length, and nothing was out of place. All was good. So then, what was he to keep? Certainly not to keep the Devil out, for he had access—even to God's throne room.

Adam was given the opportunity to name created things: "And out of the ground the LORD God formed every beast of the field, and every fowl of the air; and brought *them* unto Adam to see what he would call them: and whatsoever Adam called every living creature, that *was* the name thereof. And Adam gave names to all cattle and to the fowl of the air, and to every beast of the field" (Gen. 1:19-20a.)

This meant that beauty, exuberance, and the aptitude to appreciate was placed in him while he was being created and furthermore explains that God put Glory in his hands. Adam was the keeper of God's praise and glory, making him the crown of creation.

And He went to them in the cool of the day and had fellowship. Lucifer (*title given to Satan*), a Cherub and Maestro in charge of the praise team in Heaven, once ordered Praise, Glory, and Honor to the King of kings, the Ruler of the universe, and knew what it meant; and again, it was on that basis that he envied his Creator God.

Five times He said *I will*, showing his determination to achieve absolute glory and praise, but he was defeated. That covetous one, could not appreciate the fact that God gave the lower creature (*man*) the glorious position as Ruler of the works of His hands. Question is, What is man that he could be pure, and he who is born of humanity, and that he could be righteous?. For this man, was made of substance lower than the angels.

The fact that God breathed His breath into man and he became a living soul bewildered and distressed the Devil. Moreover, he then yearned for replication, for he thought that that masterpiece (*man, the crown of creation*) holds that which was and still is most desirable to him and that, if he had control over the man, he would get the glory. As the spirit of God fills man, so is the Devil's desire to enter in and take over his being.

The body of man is the temple of God, and therefore, evil and good cannot inhabit the same time, just as light and darkness cannot occupy the same space. For the Devil to have total control of any human being, that individual must be abhorrent of God and His knowledge. And moreover, the body was not made to house evil, which is why, when one is possessed of demons, there is disfigurement and alterations to the corporeal and emotional make up. The body must and will die of exasperation. The remuneration of depravity is death, but the love and grace of God validates eternal life.

To sin means to miss the mark of life and true spiritual union with our Creator for all eternity. From the time he was kicked out of Heaven, Satan constantly hounded for a means to sever God's relationship with man because he thought that he deserved all the glory, honor, and praise that truly belong to God. He found the woman as the means. Inquiring and all the time not knowing or understanding the lot, she was forced to notice the tree and wondered but knew the command of God, for Adam had told her.

However, her inquisitiveness got the best of her and opened the door of opportunity for the Devil to go in and sow his seed of doubt, which led to the death of man, the friend of God. His masterpiece was broken and its glory taken away.

Satan accused God of hiding the truth: "And the woman said unto the serpent, we may eat of the fruit of the trees of the garden: But of the fruit of the tree which *is* in the midst of the garden, God hath said, Ye shall not eat of it, neither shall ye touch it, lest ye die.

The serpent said unto the woman, "You shall not surely die: for God doth know that in the day you eat thereof, then your eyes shall be opened, and you shall be as gods, knowing good and evil.'

And when the woman saw that the tree *was good for food*, and that it *was* pleasant to the eyes, and a tree to be desired to *make one wise*, she took of the fruit thereof, and did eat, and gave also unto her husband with her; and he did eat.

The serpent (Satan personified) stimulated Eve's curiosity, from which he invoked the *need to know*, (**Self In Need**) with the sad result of doubting God, their Creator and friend, thus bringing about a perspective for man's reason to fail. The Creator made man to live without needs, so having needs is a transgression of His law. That is why the sinner must die.

She passed on the principle of death (*the seed is sin*) to her husband, and he did eat. Immediately, they felt the change and the effect of sinning, violating God's law. The sense of right and wrong became alive, and they were awakened to a completely new world of feelings and dependencies, consequently generating a living conscience.

Conscience is a compound faculty, the joint working of a judgment of right and wrong. The sense of obligation always follows judgment. Conscience is a whole courtroom in itself, having a Judge, Jury, Witness, with remorse as its merciless Sheriff and Chief Executioner. Reason is a faculty that inquires as to the rationale of things. That is why God said in the first place, "Do not touch." If their Creator had let them alone after sinning, they would have been reprobate, i.e., with dammed souls.

Living without God, Satan could have had total control over him, and such was the plot of the enemy of souls. At that time of life, Adam and Eve needed the Father's guidance more than ever. Consider how quickly the blood rushes to heal a laceration. The blood is life, so life rushes immediately to heal.

I can imagine how they felt at that rude awakening as their conscience came alive to give them a fighting chance for the possession of their souls. After all, as gods, they were responsible for their own lives. Nevertheless, they were about to face wars from within and without. With no experience, they prepared for the future. Let us see what happened next.

Eight

Leaves Will Not Do

They were both naked, the man and his wife, and were not ashamed (Gen. 2:25). This time of their life is known as the Dispensation of Innocence. They were clothed in righteousness and were happy as children, exploring their new world, with no cares or worries. They did what any normal human being would, but with purity in heart and with absolute obedience to their maker. Their hearts were not cluttered with obscenity, i.e., offensiveness to God's standards of decency, especially by being sexually explicit disgusting, and morally offensive and particularly through an apparent total disregard for others' rights or natural justice.

The enemy of souls watched covetously and, later, succeeded with his plot to taint creation; however, our Creator had an intention of His own. "And the eyes of them both were opened, and they knew that they *were* naked; and they sewed fig leaves together, and made themselves aprons" (Gen. 3:7).

The days of innocence came to an abrupt end, and they realized that they were naked. How sin can shed the covering off sleepy souls, revealing it to the fury of God! They just did not feel the chill of cool breeze on their skins only. Their entire being had come to consciousness or realization that they must die, and for the first time in their lives, they were afraid. Suddenly, they were on their own to fend for themselves. They did not feel close to God, for His dread was upon their conscience. They felt like babies that had just come out of the womb and inhaling their first breathe of fresh air. The warmth and comfort of the sack that they were in was gone. They felt safe no more and could only cry, but crying was not enough; they needed comfort, love, cuddling, and shelter from the elements.

Fig leaves were not enough to cover or ease the pain and discomfort resulting from their sins. The sinner cannot use perfunctory (*matter of duty*) or carnal means to hide and eradicate transgressions. God's plan of salvation does not come about by one becoming a god, creating his own terms and conditions. He is the only wise God our Savior, to who *are* glory and majesty, dominion and power, both now and ever (Jude 1:25).

The Devil's sinister plot was revealed when he told Eve that their eyes will be open, and that they would not die but would be as gods, knowing good and evil. It was his intention to become God.

They tried to invent a covering, yet the voice of God (*represents His will*) was far more powerful, for they heard it walking in the Garden. The leaves here are an allegory to the law interpreted by man. Satan knew that man was made to depend upon his Creator in order to live (*faith*), so he crafted the scheme of doubt that led to disobedience so that he (*man*) could try and live on his own (i.e., *without God*).

Keep in mind that gods have power to create. Therefore, the first thing created by the new self-made gods was a covering, the means of hiding from God's judgment and to satiate their conscience. The abrupt and punitive experience of their new habitat coupled with remorse, I do believe, fostered dislike to been gods, but needed help. God had the answer to the trouble they had gotten themselves into. Ashamed, helpless and afraid, Adam and Eve hid themselves.

Many think they can sin or violate God's law with no consequence. But know this, the sin not confessed, forsaken and forgiven never goes unpunished. You may ask again, "Why *did God not stop this* from continuing?" The answer is found in the law of sowing and reaping. Seeds sown in the ground will not be taken out and put aside. Man is given a sovereign will from his maker, and with that will, he must choose to do right or wrong. He was on probation.

God created time for everything on the earth to come to fruition, and these characters are now at hand, not in eternity. At that juncture, time was given for the seed of sin to grow, ripen, and be picked. That is the law of nature, but the Creator prepared these occurrences on this approach to bring about the final defeat of the Devil. The first Adam was an archetype, and the true Adam was and is Jesus. Therefore, the first man Adam was designed to fail.

God went on the scene and as a caring father would, made coats of skins and clothed them (Gen. 3:21). The hand of the one and only righteous God made a *true* covering for them. He killed a lamb, maybe two, and made the covering. Here is the application: The Lamb slain and its skin used for a covering is a type of Christ's blood that cleanses man from sins and clothes him in righteousness, making him approachable to God. It was not aprons that cover a portion but coats that cover all. We read of the lamb slain from the foundation of the world (Rev. 13:8).

Grace intervened, and mercy rewrote man's life. Instead of the death sentence that the Devil contemplated for the creature called man, God curved it to be a promise of hope, thus making Him faithful to His Word. Be reminded that there are two deaths. The first death is the physical death, that is, when the spirit leaves the body. The second is spiritual (*eternal death*); this is when the soul is debarred from the presence of God forever and ever into darkness.

The Devil thought of eternally separating man form his Creator, and he could not know the mind of God as to why man was made lower (*of the earth*) than the angels but crowned with His Glory! Nor could he place a value on time, since he only knew of eternity. "But God hath chosen the foolish things of the world to confound the wise; and God hath chosen the weak things of the world to confound the things which are mighty; And base things of the world, and things which are despised, hath God chosen, *yea*, and things which are not, to bring to naught things that are" (1 Cor. 1:27-28).

The wise here is the master of evil, the father of lies, called Satan. The base thing is that man has been made a little lower than the angels (*of the earth*). Satan despised the promises of God, for he of himself cannot make or keep any, and to him, they are of no value. Well! They would not help him anyway; he is incapable of repenting or redeemed, but he is doomed for eternal death.

At this point, the Omnipotent God mystified him with a plan to undo the evil done to man, and certainly not gave a specific time for this to come to pass.

The seed of sin was sown, and like any other sown seed, it must germinate, grow, mature, and bear fruit. The fruit must then mature, ripen, and then be picked. After the tree has borne its season, it goes through the autumn, winter, and then spring again to bear more fruit. In autumn, the leaves fall, and the tree seems to die, but afterward comes winter, where it sleeps (*a kin to death*). With the substance of life and the regeneration ability, which God the Creator puts in the earth, the tree awakens at springtime with new buds ready to bear fruit.

In addition, it is so that God created time for everything to come to completion, for that is the fundamentals of time (Gen. 8:22). Now in order for man to live again, the seed of life must be sown, germinated, grown, ripened, and preferred, but this time, it will be on the soil of death, with Jesus Christ in God our eternal hope.

Apostle Paul endured all the enemy could throw at him even the kitchen sink missed, but for the chosen's sakes that they may also receive the salvation which is in Christ Jesus with eternal glory. Everything God made was good, and still is, and those good things that last forever, bring glory and honor. Satan does not have the ability to create; he is titled, the destroyer.

And as the agent and Prince of darkness, he goes about only to steal God's glory, kill, and *destroy* anyone in his way, for that is his nature. But Jesus came to give life more abundantly.

Satan coveted the glory given to man. So an everlasting dispute is here instigated between the sovereignty of God and the realm of the Devil, along with men; antagonism (hostility) is declared stuck between the seed of the woman and the germ of the serpent.

It took eons of time for Satan to become the master of evil, lies, pride, adversary and deception. Therefore, man made a little lower than the angels was no match for him, and for God to use the base things of the earth to confound this wise and prudent being, humankind had to be subjugated (*under control*).

This war that began in Heaven between Michael and the dragon is the fruit of this enmity: (1) that there is a continual conflict between grace and corruption in the hearts of God's people. Satan, by their (men's) corruptions, assaults them, buffets them, sifts them, and seeks to devour them, (2) they, by the exercise of their graces, resist him, wrestle with him, quench his fiery darts, and force him to flee from them. Heaven and hell can never be reconciled nor can light and darkness and no more can Satan and a sanctified soul, for these are contrary to one another.

Thanks be to God, there is a bliss set before us, and a tree of life in the midst of it, which we must rejoice in the hopes of entering. Remember the Angels were set to keep the way to the tree of life which hitherto Adam and Eve had been in; that is, it was henceforward in vain for he and his seed to expect righteousness, life, and happiness, by virtue of the first covenant, for it was irreparably broken, and could never be pleaded, nor any benefit taken by it. The command of that covenant being broken, the curse of it is in full force; it leaves no room for repentance, but we are all undone if we be judged by that covenant. God revealed this to Adam, not to drive him to despair, but to oblige and quicken him to look for life and happiness in the promised seed, by whom the flaming sword is removed. God and his angels are reconciled to us, and a new and living way into the holiest is consecrated and laid open for us.

Nine

Only the Best Will Do

In due time, Eve bore two sons; the first was Cain and the second Abel. Adam's sons learned to worship God and offer sacrifices to Him; Abel's sacrifice was accepted but Cain's rejected. The scripture records, "Not as Cain, *who* was of that wicked one, and slew his brother. And wherefore slew he him? Because his own works were evil, and his brother's righteous. Marvel not, my brethren, if the world hate you" (1 John 2:12).

Here the first Son was the son of the fallen nature, and the second is of the righteous and the battle of good and evil continues, for Cain killed his brother. The seed of sin is now ripe and ideal. At this time, Satan again thought that Abel must have been the seed who would bruise his head (or would stem from his lineage), so in order to avert his own defeat, he forced the killing of the righteous. We should not be alarmed when we go through trials, for the enemy of souls never rests.

Please note that it is important to educate from conception, for the child in the womb is inherent of every emotion and impression conceived. Let us understand also that each sacrifice of atonement was a type of the crucifixion of Jesus Christ, the crucial sacrifice for our sins. Abel gave to God the first calf, and God said, "Thou shalt set apart unto the LORD all that open the uterus and (Exod. 13:12)

The first speaks of Christ: "But now is Christ risen from the dead, and become the *first fruits* of them that slept. But every man in his own order: Christ the *first fruits*; afterward they that are Christ's at his coming" (1 Cor. 15:20. 23). Blood had to be shed, for it is life and the only way back to God.

Life must be given, not taken. "And almost all things are by the law purged with blood; and without shedding of blood is no remission" (Heb. 9:22).

The first calf is the pure strength produced from the source and must be preserved.

It is paradoxical that Abel was not the first, but Cain, showing that sin will be setting the pace, and righteousness will follow to purify. However, let sin take its course, for it is certain it will come to an end. The tree will fall, and where it falls, there shall it lie until judgment takes its course. The commandments were not yet given to man, but how did Abel know that he should have given the best, which was the firstling, to God? The firstling is the promise of future posterity, and to sacrifice it would be considered unwise. Nevertheless, as a man of faith, he trusted in God and believed that He would bless Him with more.

Abel had the righteous seed in him, and it was therefore natural for him to give the best to his Creator. The Devil coveted the praise and respect that God gave to Abel and thought that he carried the seed that would eventually bruise his heel; so killing him was to appease the vehemence.

Here is the application: The fruit from the cursed will not atone for redemption. Cain's fruit was of the ground, which shows that Satan also wanted to frustrate God's plan for redemption by substituting pure blood with the accursed. Product of the curse cannot produce the cure. The fruit was used to tempt Eve; nonetheless, it sadly caused Adam to fall. To redeem them, life would have to be given, not taken, and because of Adam's fall, all are subjected to death (*the dreaded state and place*).

Only the best was accepted. "Moreover, in process of time, it happened that Cain brought of the fruit of the ground an offering unto the LORD. And Abel, he also brought of the first of his flock and of the fat also. And the LORD had respect unto Abel and to his offering: But unto Cain and to his offering he had not respect. And Cain was very wroth, and his countenance fell. And the LORD said unto Cain, Why art thou wroth?

Adam never knew, or needed sexual pleasures with his wife Eve while they were in Eden, because they were not depending on the flesh for their happiness. David wrote in Psalm 16:11, "Thou wilt show me the path of life: in thy presence *is* fullness of joy; at thy right hand *there are* pleasures for evermore."

They experienced pleasures with the fullness of joys far above the sensuality of mortality, reminding us that we can live a victorious life over sin. You see, the flesh has its dictates and adhering laws interpreted as needs. Oh, how these needs are overpowering! It is upon this demeanor that Satan seizes control by means of man's desires and maliciously orders each move or actions.

You may wonder why Adam's sons were so different in nature. Let me explain: the seed of righteousness was sown (i.e., *the Word of God*) in Eve the day she was created, for Adam had told her. The Serpent followed to sow the seed of sin on the fertile ground, her mind, by way of doubt. Hence the expression, "You are what you eat." Eve was not cautious to guard her heart.

Solomon wrote, "Keep thy heart with all diligence; for out of it *are* the issues of life. Put away from thee a forward mouth, and perverse lips put far from thee. Let thine eyes look right on, and let thine eyelids look straight before thee. Ponder the path of thy feet, and let all thy ways be established. Turn not to the right hand nor to the left" (Prov. 4:23-27a).

Both seeds germinated in due course and produced Cain and Abel. Cain was the product of evil, and his name meant "acquired spear." Abel was the product of good, and his name meant "breath or vapor." He was called so probably because of the shortness of his life. The first false religion is adept by the first son, resulting in the first murder. Cain's blinded rage prevented him from considering his position as the head and ruler of his brother. For God said it in this wise: "Unto you shall be his desire." He was the firstborn.

The seed of iniquity that was *transferred* from the serpent had played its part. The firstborn receives the greater portion of inheritance. Cain could not be satisfied with his birthright, and this was Satan's quarrel in Heaven. The evil spirit here desired to have its way, for God said, "Sin lay at the door of his heart." It was a deliberate attempt by the forces of darkness to taint the worship and praise for God and to provoke Him to forsake man so that it (*sin*) could rule over him.

We should love one another, not as Cain who killed his brother. And why did he kill him? It was because; his own workings were from an evil heart, while his brother's work from a righteous heart.

Ten

Satan's Engagement with Man

Although the earth was also cursed, it could not willingly receive innocent blood, so the blood of Abel cried out to God for vengeance, and He pronounced the sentence on Cain to be a vagabond (drifter) just like the Devil in Job 1:7: "And the LORD said unto Satan, Whence comest thou? Then Satan answered the LORD, and said, From going to and fro in the earth, and from walking up and down in it."

A mark for death was set on him by God, and anyone who saw him was to kill him, but the love of God, which is so great afar than tongue or pen could ever tell, that goes beyond the highest star and reaches to the lowest hell, touched Cain, for he groaned and said that his punishment was more than he could bear.

God could not despise the cry of his penance, so mercy rewrote Cain's life. God said that "Anyone who kills him, vengeance would be taken on him seven times." Satan could not get forgiveness for his iniquities, so I can imagine the look on his face when Cain left God's presence. I further believe that Satan feared the Word of God, so he ceased from trying to kill Cain. O! What peace we often forfeit! O! What needless pain we bear! All because we do not carry everything to God in prayer.

Cain quickly left his home and the voice of God as a fugitive and a vagabond with a visible mark impressed on him for death. He was the seed of iniquity, and if anyone saw him, he was to kill him, but his death should be recompensed seven times. This tells us that we must hate sin as much as God does, and it does not matter who the sinner is. A signal is here given to man on how to get back to fellowship with his Creator.

The sign was revealed in the type of offering through faith from Abel (*remember he gave the firstling, the male*). By faith Abel offered unto God a more excellent sacrifice than Cain, by which he obtained witness that he was righteous, God testifying of his gifts: and by it he being dead his blood spoke" (Heb. 11:4). Much like forensics used nowadays in connection with the detection of crime to determine guilt or innocence.

By this time, Satan had already claimed territory and predetermined to continue the war that started in Heaven, by controlling mankind through their weaknesses, dictating their every move, with the intention to lead them in rebellion against God. His relationship to man has been that of a commander-in-chief, working swiftly in corrupting their thoughts, exciting and heightening their senses to the burning desire called unlawful lust (i.e., to hanker after, yearn).

Lust affects the emotions in a complete and irresistible way. It is overwhelming and overpowering to so great an extent or degree that it breeds reverential fear, thus nurturing worship. For example, when Goliath yelled at the Israelites, they feared (give reverence) and hid in dens and holes.

We are commanded not to have any other gods besides the only true Almighty God, for that which we fear or depend on are revered and become god. "For thou shalt worship no other god: for the LORD, whose name *is* Jealous, *is* a jealous God. Fear God and keep His commandments for this is the whole duty of man" (Eccles. 12). The furthermost important task of Satan in the midst of men now is to fake the rule or principle that forms the basis of our faith, theory, or policy and experiences of God as discovered in scripture in order to deceive the saints (2 Cor. 11:14-15; Eph. 6:10-18; Luke 10:18).

We are further commanded to confirm and analyze all teachings and doctrines in the spiritual sphere to distinguish if they are of God or Satan (1 Cor. 2:12-16; Phil. 1:9-10; 1 Thess. 5:21-22).

It is certain that not every religious conviction, dogma, and practice can be of God. For that reason, we must judge them with the Word of God.

Comprehension of the validity of God's Word is the first crucial factor in warfare against demons and errors. Satan uses every imaginable resource to hold men in weakness to him and keeps them from approaching God. If he fails in this, he tries to destroy the believer's evidence and reduce to rubble his authority in God. If a Christian stumbles and drops from God's standard of living, he attempts to pin him down in order to keep him fallen or even to the point of committing suicide. He hides the fact that this is only the beginning of real suffering in a never-ending hell.

Satan's strategy here is to get the Child of God in a halfhearted state of affairs and plead with him by silent whispers to stay in that condition, with the intention that God would erase him from the Book of Life. If they do not go wanton (*uncalled-for pleasures*), he organizes schemes for people to believe they are lacking everything in life and lays emphasis on indulgence and aberrant pleasures as candid delights, while provoking defiant passions, and disposes them of all self-control to live carousingly.

God's purpose for allowing the Devil to continue is to develop character and faith in His child. Blessings, with a crown of life, await those that endure temptation. Know that, the trial of your faith, stands much more precious than gold that can loose its luster and value, though it be strained with fire, may be found unto praise and honor and glory at the coming of Jesus Christ:

The Prophets who prophesied of grace, have enquired and searched diligently of what time the Spirit of grace the unmerited favor would come upon fallen man.

But, believers are fortunate to experience God's abundant grace in these last days that began on the day of Pentecost when 120 disciples were filled with the Holy Ghost.

Unto whom it was revealed, that not unto themselves, but unto us they did minister the things, which are now reported unto you by them that have preached the gospel unto you with the Holy Ghost sent down from heaven; which things the angels desire to look into. Wherefore gird up the loins of your mind, be sober, and hope to the end for the grace that is to be brought unto you at the revelation of Jesus Christ (1 Pet. 1:12-13).

Satan does not appreciate the important attribute of integrity, for he does not possess it. He had the chance when he was Lucifer but fell: He is already defeated, so let us not be distressed at the fiery trials, for such will prove us worthy and truly build godly character in us. "Beloved, think it not strange concerning the fiery trial which is to try you, as though some strange thing happened unto you: But rejoice, inasmuch as ye are partakers of Christ's sufferings; that, when his glory shall be revealed, ye may be glad also with exceeding joy" (1 Pet. 4:12-13).

The souls that were born again and ravaged by the enemy over the years are earmarked to inherit the kingdom that Satan lost. We are heirs and joint heirs with Christ who now reigns supreme, and we will be in power with Him. Please note that this position was and still is what Satan hunts, subsequently, to seize by force. He (*Satan*) now uses the knowledge of good and evil, compounded with the idea of man becoming a god, to manipulate and control them.

Therefore, the flesh befalls to fascination by means of its senses that are heightened to uncontrollable propensity, consequently missing the mark of holiness. There is a way, which seems right unto a man, but the end thereof *is* the ways of death" (Prov. 14:12).

Eleven

Bags of Burdens

Here is a good spot to reveal some of the workings of Satan. The Lord gave me this vision: I was at the bottom of a sea that was dirty and overcast, as when a storm is eminent and the wind blows dust and things around, or, as when snow is falling and visibility is low. *This sea of forgetfulness,* so called from the beginning of time, was not deep because "Bags of Burdens" that humankind threw away from since its foundation piled on one another. Remembering when I was a child in Sunday school, we sang this song:

> *"Never to be remembered anymore, Jesus cast my burden of sins today, Into the sea of forgetfulness, never to be remembered any more, For they are gone, gone, gone, gone, yes! My sins are gone, buried in the deepest sea Yes it's good enough for me, I shall live, eternally, praise God my sins are gone."*

In the vision, I was at the bottom without any diving gear (*the Spirit caused me to breathe*). There, in the sullied water, I saw a tall, distinguished, slim but well-built man, dressed in a business suit, as he jumped in the sea, but the water was not disturbed. In the meanwhile, many people threw bags of burdens therein that kept coming down around us, as when rain is falling.

The businessman was a dealer of antiquity (i.e., finding value in relics, refuse, and junk. And with industry and frustration, he quickly took up a bag (*for it was his trade*) and flew out of the sea where on the shore stood the former owner, a man known as the penitent, was free and relieved of his burden of sins. We simultaneously got on the shore.

He had just left the presence of God, a former sinner but now saved by grace, for all his sins that were forgiven were thrown into the sea of forgetfulness (*he carried them in the bag*).

Satan the businessperson, also called the deceiver, went quickly to the man with an angry countenance and bewilderment at why he had thrown those things away. He assiduously opened and displayed the contents of the bag to the man in order to appeal to the conscience, while he was in moral cognition. The bag contained the sum of sins and past actions of the carnal man (*an enmity against God*); though the items in the bag were small, carrying it over the years became unbearable.

You see, the soul was not created to sin or miss the mark, so carrying out that task every day brought about remorse and shame; hence the cry of the soul for freedom. One cannot run a race with weights, for such is life. Apostle Paul wrote about war in the members of the body and the mind is the battlefield (Rom. 7:18-22).

We must lay aside every weight and the sin, which doth so easily beset us in order to compete. In the bag were—(1) *a bar of soap*, (2) *a toothbrush*, and (3) *a quarter (25 cents)* and other things that were used as instruments for life's comfort and protection. Each item had a devout control, submission, and interpretation. This business is to appeal to the man while his heart was contrite but covetously to keep the soul in bondage. The dealer thought sadly that it was necessary for evil to work immediately.

For the penitent is a newborn babe in Christ and, therefore, must be broken while he is young, tender, and susceptible. Sadly, though, each item had its specific stronghold on the man.

The soap and the toothbrush represent personal sanitation and could only cleanse temporarily, but the Devil crafted it to be of lifelong necessity. David wrote in Psalm 51:5, 6: "Behold, I was shaped in iniquity; and in sin did my mother conceive me. Behold, thou desires truth in the inward parts: and in the hidden *part* thou shalt make me to know wisdom."

These important items are used daily by mankind, (*because the body generates sin and corruption constantly*), and are used to cleanse the body for general acceptance among the fellows only. However, wretchedly, they aid in disguising the truth about the condition of the soul. If one feels absolutely clean and accepted in the social order (*Satan said*), he is deceived to think that there's no need for the Spirit's cleansing. We cannot ignore the fact that we are clean through the words that are spoken by Christ.

However, only the Holy Spirit shows what habits to forsake, and what society to relinquish and convicts of wrong.

The soap and toothbrush are a direct cryptogram, i.e., secret code, of false hope and religion that makes a man think his ways are right and that his own righteousness and works are good. The saying goes, "If it feels good, it can't be bad," thus causing the sinner to rely on his own works to save him.

The scripture says that there is a way that seems right unto a man, but the end thereof is the ways of death. God also said, "But we are all as an unclean *thing*, and all our righteousness *are* as filthy rags; and we all do fade as a leaf; and our iniquities, like the wind, have taken us away."

As the soap was used, it got thinner, and the sinner, realizing that it is not good enough to keep him clean always, discarded it, so the Devil quickly retrieved it (*like the retriever dog*) to offer the believer. The child of God must be persistent in his prayer life and devotion.

He must be even more importunate in throwing habits away, for such perseverance will surely cause the desire for things to diminish, the same as the soap, thus having no appeal or stronghold.

Therefore, while receiving the word of truth, the penitent is awakened to the reality that he is not clean enough to stand before God his Father and needs to pray and fast for cleansing. Nevertheless, to reestablish the unfruitful works of darkness, Satan forever lies in wait, until the repentant leaves the presence of the Lord. The penitent was coerced to make the choice of accepting false religion or to resist, in order for the Devil to flee. However, when the soap had no appeal to the penitent, Satan had nothing more to use. So he left him. Satan can only tempt because of what is inside us, i.e., the things we crave.

Whatever you do, please persevere, and do not stop praying. Spiritual battles are won through being on the knees in prayer constantly.

The quarter (25 cents) represents false hope and security. "For the love of money is the root of all evil: which while some coveted after, they have erred from the faith, and pierced themselves through with many sorrows" (1 Tim. 6:10).

The power to afford everything the flesh desires gives grounds for individuals not to depend on God to supply their needs and ultimately blinded to see no motivation of having faith. We read in Hebrews 11, "That if one has no faith, God has no pleasure in him and without faith, it is impossible to please Him, for he that cometh to God must believe that he is and that he is a rewarder of them that diligently seek Him."

So here the Devil bargained with the man and said, "It is only a quarter. With it, you were able to get to a dollar and bought everything you needed; after all, money answered all things as the scripture says." He went on to say that "God did not want him to suffer and be in need. The quarter is harmless."

You must understand that the penitent is a novice to the scriptures, so he had no defense against this master of time and deception. In Matthew, Chapter 4, note how Jesus handled temptation: in every instance, He used the written word, and the tempter left Him.

The Devil insisted that money is not evil, (*but the word says it's the love thereof*), and in order to be satisfied, you will need to get more and more. *Jesus said, "The love of money is the root of all evil."* Gaining the amount of a dollar is necessary, then on to a hundred, argued the deceiver.

Satan went on to say that, "Man was cursed to work (*even robbery is considered a career*), and God helps those who help themselves," thus exciting the passion to lust for more and, consequently, instilling the need for man to be contingent, not on God. He also said that the dollar made him a survivor.

Now, faith is the property of things anticipated, without which it is impossible to please God. (Heb. 11:1). If there is nothing in you to use, Satan cannot tempt you, on the other hand you cannot be tempted with nothing. Therefore, he has to re-introduce all that is familiar to the soul, and with the acceptance thereof, he shackles the individual, and this is the answer to the question on "Why do people repeat the same sins over and over?"

"Be sober, be vigilant; because your adversary the devil, as a roaring lion, walked about, seeking whom he may devour: Whom resist steadfast in the faith, knowing that the same afflictions are accomplished in your brethren that are in the world. But the God of all grace, who hath called us unto his eternal glory by Christ Jesus, after that ye have suffered a while, make you perfect, establish, strengthen, settle *you*" (1 Pet. 5:8-10).

We now continue where we left off. Then men began to call upon the name of God. Evil is relentless in its pursuit to destroy Good. As time turned over, men multiplied, and the evil eyes of Satan began hunting on for the promised one that would crush his head. He thought it was Job and that is why he was so prosperous and well-protected. Therefore, in order to prove that man was nothing, the evil one moved the Father to trouble him.

Note this: even though Satan polluted man's heart, God kept the good seed (the promised Messiah) hidden for the appropriate time, and the accuser had no knowledge of it.

The story of Job depicts how God invisibly protects the man of uprightness, integrity and faith.

Hast not thou made a hedge about him, and about his house, and about all that he hath on every side? Thou hast blessed the work of his hands, and his substance increased in the land" (Job 1:8-11). Job's heart was set on doing righteousness, and it pleased God that he taught his children, thus preserving the word, the path, and the seed of good for man's redemption. As time went on, we see the Devil invented ways to destroy man; he so corrupted the earth, till it moved God to devastate a world (*in the time of Noah*), saving only eight souls, and then Sodom and Gomorrah, saving only four souls.

Man, made from the dust of the earth, a little lower than the angels, crowned with God's glory and given dominion over creation, is still coveted by the fiend, a disgraced cherubim that constantly pines for power, worship, and praise. As the seeds sown in good soil develop to produce, so is the father of lies and inventor of evil. He must run his course until God gets ready to remove him.

The path back to Eden is now long and obscure. It seems that all interest is lost, or is it? God has not forgotten. He honors His Word above His very name. He said, "Till Heaven and earth pass, one jot or tittle shall in no wise pass from the law till all be fulfilled" (Matt. 5:18). He predestinated certain men (*e.g., the patriarchs*) as head of the household, and to them were committed the word of promise (*covenant*) to command and teach their children and future generations, for the enemy had weakened their integrity.

"And the patriarchs moved with envy, sold Joseph into Egypt: but God was with him" (Acts 7:9). Moreover, when the Fathers failed, God rose up prophets to bear the awesome burden of delivering and interpreting His Word and live triumphantly over evil and sin. They were the oracles (*divine answer to question*) of God, for He could not walk on the earth anymore because it was polluted. Man must lead his race back to God.

Satan's kingdom was threatened, for there were more men, which could not be manipulated or swayed by his cunning schemes. So he wreaked havoc, confused the populace, and inflamed tortures, killing, and imprisonment of those chosen men of God.

Nevertheless, the light did not go out, for each prophet of God was compelled to convey *the word* to the people (*even in perils*) so that hope could remain. God preferred a nation through whom to speak to the world and carry the torch that would keep the flames that light the way (the Christian race) to Eternity. They were given the commandments, i.e., God's ordinance, for righteous living.

The tabernacle was instated to teach reverence, dedication, and faith. Numbers 16:9 says, "Is it a small thing to you that the God of Israel has separated you from the congregation of Israel, to bring you near to Himself, to do the work of the *tabernacle of the Lord,* and to stand before the congregation to serve them?" The sacrifices, the Priests, and Levites were instituted by God so that man could live by faith and absolute trust and reliance on Him and in His Word. The fruit of righteousness must mature and be presented to the master for His use.

I say that God will yet get the glory, and Satan will certainly be defeated. We are no match for his shrewdness, but God has made a way for us to overcome him. Satan cannot take God out of our hearts; therefore, we will have to deny Him willingly. The Ten Commandments interpret moral living.

The tabernacle speaks of the place of worship where Jehovah dwells; it also signifies that our heart is the ideal place of worship. Note the cleanliness of it and the type of furniture and arrangements, the attendants, their attire, dedication, consecration, and lifestyle.

The Holy of Holies was where the Shekinah glory of God dwelled. In this place, only the High Priest used to go once a year to make atonement for the people and himself—a type of Christ, the only one qualified, to be in the awesome presence of God the Father.

The Ark of the Covenant *contained* the Ten Commandments (Deut. 10:4, 5), Aaron's rod (Num. 17:10; Heb. 9:4), and the pot of manna that portrayed the Word of God and always remained fresh (Exod. 16:33, 34). It was conveyed by the Levites (Num. 3:30, 31) on a cart (1 Sam. 6:7-15) before Israel (Josh. 3:3-17) into battle (1 Sam. 4:4, 5). Its purposes were as follows: it was a symbol of God's Law (Exod. 25:16, 21), a memorial of God's provision (Exod. 16:33, 34), a place to know God's will (Exod. 25:22; 30:6, 36), a place of entreaty (Josh. 7:6-15), a symbol of God's holiness (1 Sam. 6:19; 2 Sam. 6:6, 7), a place of atonement (Lev. 16:2, 14-17), and a symbol of Heaven (Rev. 11:19). The Tabernacle was ordained on Mount Sinai (Exod. 33:7-11).

Moses took the Tabernacle and pitched it without the camp, afar from the camp, and called it the Tabernacle of the congregation. And it came to pass *that* every one that sought the LORD went out unto the tabernacle of the congregation, which *was* without the camp.

And it came to pass, when Moses went out unto the tabernacle that all the people rose up and stood every man *at* his tent door and looked after Moses until he was gone into the tabernacle. And it came to pass that as Moses entered into the tabernacle, the cloudy pillar descended and stood *at* the door of the tabernacle, and *the LORD* talked with Moses.

And all the people saw the cloudy pillar stand *at* the tabernacle door, and all the people rose up and worshipped, every man *in* his tent door.

"And the LORD spake unto Moses face to face, as a man speaketh unto his friend. And he turned again into the camp, but his servant Joshua, the son of Nun, a young man, departed not out of the tabernacle" (Exod. 33:11). "And let them make me a sanctuary; that I may dwell among them" (Exod. 25:8).

Under the Old Testament system of atonement, the blood of beasts (heifers, bullocks, lambs, rams) was offered as sacrifice at the tabernacle for sins. The animal had to be perfect if the Lord was to accept the burnt offering. As all the sacrifices were consumed on the altar, an offering made in this way was a pleasant savor to the Lord.

The priests had specific instructions from the Lord on the slaughter of animals as to how to kill the offering, sprinkle the blood on the altar, and burn incense (censer) in order to atone for the sins of the people. Sacrifices had to be made continually, although such regulations were only a shadow of the things to come.

Twelve

The Temperament of Things

All things are created for God's glory. All things were made with specific purposes and grandeur. All things remain consistent with its original nature. The flowers have their splendor, and they still remain the same; all insects have their purposes, and they were made with their wonder and remain the same.

Why did God make man with His own two hands and gave him a nature that could fall, yet crowned him with His glory and made him keeper over the works of His hands? Was it to keep enemies out, or to keep animals from destroying the vegetation, or perhaps to trim hedges? No!

You must see that God made everything perfect; nothing grew out of order. All animals eat grass, and the grass grows to acceptable heights; the keeper has nothing to do but live and enjoy creation.

Let us look at the title (*his job description*) "Keeper" of the garden. This means to maintain and ensure that things remain the same as the Creator made them, i.e., to uphold the glory and praise of the Creator. God placed the law of appreciation in alignment with man, making him a son.

Lucifer's name meant, "son of the morning" or "morning star." God made beings and things for special purposes. Each has its duty.

Whether to shine, look beautiful, sing, rule, guard, carry messages, or uphold standards, God made it so. Satan lost his illustrious position because of pride.

In the beginning, God created man in His own image, and he fell from grace. But for now, he had to be content with being a little lower than the angels; yet he possessed great abilities with passion, whilst experience molded him into perfection.

He was created to make God's praise glorious. Adam named everything and such as it is, being what they were; however, he could not have done that unless God deposited reason within him. He furthermore placed the creative ability in man, with the power to choose.

1 Corinthians 14 says, "And that he might make known the riches of his glory on the vessels of mercy, which he had afore prepared unto glory, for of him, and through him, and to him, are all things: to whom be glory forever. Wherefore receive ye one another, as Christ also received us to the glory of God. Out of the mouths of babes and suckling thou hast perfected praise."

Everything that God made was for His glory, and He will get the praise. "But God hath chosen the foolish things of the world, to confound the wise; and God hath chosen the weak things of the world to confound the things which are mighty; And base things of the world, and things which are despised, hath God chosen, *yea*, and things which are not, to bring to nought things that are: That no flesh should glory in his presence" (1 Cor. 1:27-29). This scripture substantiates that God created time apart from eternity to bring about an end to unfavorable beginnings.

The wise speaks of the Devil that will be defeated by man, whom he deems foolish. A baby is imperfect because it has not matured, but God will use whomever He wills to accomplish His purpose. He also said that if man stops praising Him, then "the very stones would immediately cry out" (Luke 19:40). "But of him are ye in Christ Jesus, who of God is made unto us wisdom, and righteousness, and sanctification, and redemption: That, according as it is written, He that glorieth, let him glory in the Lord" (1 Cor. 1:28-31).

This is why the student Adam fell from grace; he wanted instant wisdom to make him a god, for gods who know good and evil also get glory and praise. Satan tricked them into thinking similar to himself, with the intention of making them to seek their own path, away from the Creator.

Satan rules this world as the mighty one, and it's in his nature to steal the praises and glory that belong to God; so persuading man to think of himself more highly than he should will make him his follower. He won over some renegade angels:

"And the angels who kept not their first estate but left their own habitation, he hath reserved in everlasting chains under darkness unto the judgment of the great day;

"They did not care for their original domain (their own principality) and did not remain in their own sphere and general habitat but left them so as to enter into the human realm and marry the daughters of men in an attempt to wipe out the untainted race from Adam and to frustrate the seed of the woman that would defeat him in due course" (Jude 6; Gen. 6:1-4).

Satan has legions of fallen angels that are now demons, i.e., disembodied spirits, to do his dirty work.

Some have set themselves as gods, ruling in every area of man's life. There are gods of sicknesses, wars, diseases, and poverty. In addition, there are gods of habits and of the flesh, with many more that are too numerous to write; however, we do see their manifestations and works. Jesus was wounded for our transgressions, and by His stripes we were healed. Every god has been defied by the children of God, except the last one that is actively ruling: the God of the flesh.

You see, the flesh will exalt itself, if given the opportunity. The wise God made man with unconventional behavior, and for this reason, he fell, in order that Jesus Christ the righteous could come and defeat the Devil through His suffering and death.

Man has become a formidable opponent of the Devil, for he has received the gift of eternal life, along with the anointing that destroys yokes, through faith in Jesus Christ.

"And it shall come to pass in that day, *that* his burden shall be taken away from off thy shoulder, and his yoke from off thy neck, and the yoke shall be destroyed because of the anointing" (Isa. 10:27). "But the anointing which ye have received of him abideth in you, and ye need not that any man teach you: but as the same anointing teacheth you of all things, and is truth, and is no lie, and even as it hath taught you, ye shall abide in him" (1 John 2:27).

The Devil does not have faith in God; he is the father of lies and wants to destroy every child of God that has the testimony of Jesus Christ and His anointing on their life. The anointing that delegates authority, and enables the child of God to do work, and cannot confer on an evil being. Moreover, the war will prolong, but whosoever will, let him come and drink of the water of life freely. "But ye shall receive power, after that the Holy Ghost is come upon you: and ye shall be witnesses unto me both in Jerusalem, and in all Judea, and in Samaria, and unto the uttermost part of the earth" (Acts 1:8).

Thirteen

What in Hell Do You Want?

Soon I was in a vision (*I was in a hospital, awaiting surgery*) and in the spirit world, where I saw hideous creatures coming at me (*I was traveling through the midst of them*). They were nauseatingly repulsive. If I were not in a trance, then certainly I would have expelled everything that was in my stomach, until there was nothing left. While passing through their territory, I saw how they control and manipulate humans. The statures of these fallen angels called demons were gigantic and overpowering.

I saw what appeared to be a woman, as the skin slowly fell off her face, one piece at a time. To my surprise, instead of flesh and bones, she was made of iron. I was greatly troubled and sorrowful, seeing many more people, as they were overtaken and possessed by the beings. Some turned into wood, others to copper, brass, and some a mixture of various materials, somewhat like the image that King Nebuchadnezzar had set up for the people to worship.

The people in my vision were once human beings but later possessed by demons but still appeared as people on the outside. Even children had been possessed. Now, the possession of children is an excessive illegal action by the Devil, for it is against the law of God for the innocent to be taken control of. Hence the term pedophile.

The reason for this kind of takeover by the Devil is to prevent the Word of God from penetrating hearts. Inert (*dead*) material cannot experience human emotions. That is why God made man a living soul, i.e., body, soul, and spirit. Our Creator God will only move upon a living heart of flesh.

He said in Ezekiel 11:19. "And I will give them one heart, and I will put a new spirit within you; and I will take the stony heart out of their flesh, and will give them an heart of flesh."

Afterward, the Spirit took me to a place under the earth, where I saw other ferocious demons that had wormlike shapes, with no heart. Their skins (*scaly and impenetrable*) were made of priceless jewels of all description and colors. A single scale could make a man very rich. The scales, however, were extremely noxious. One touch would kill, and to get a piece of their valuable skins, you would have to be turned into one of them.

Whether it was rocks, iron, copper, wood, or anything, it was easy for them as they tunneled. They were unstoppable. In the midst of those creatures, I saw the face and body of a friend of mine, who had been transformed to be one of them. The sight made me very sad because my friend is marked for death and hell, i.e., eternal separation from God.

Similar to the worm-like creatures, she had no heart and, as a result, no feelings; consequentially, she had become an individual on the way to eternal damnation. In order to be saved, the heart's door must be open for the Master to come in and sup. Therefore, if an individual has no heart, no entrance but ultimate doom. The entrance of the word of God gives light and life. God's word *is also* alive, and powerful, and sharper than any double-edged sword, earsplitting even in-between soul and spirit, and of the connections and core, and *is* a discerner of the deliberations and purposes of your heart. The tour went on for a great while, for I was in a trance, and my guide interpreted the scenes to my mind.

We came upon an old castle that had a cloud hovering over it that poured rain constantly. At the entrance, there was a very long line of people interconnected by means of a very large chain with hooks forced deep into their flesh. The hooks were placed on parts of their bodies according to the nature of their sins.

Let me explain: when a person steals, the hands are used to perpetrate the crime, so the huge hooks were placed in that part of the body. Hooks with chains were placed in mouths, sides of heads, in the stomach, in the jaws, in the chest where the heart is, and in just about every part you could think of that can be used to commit sin.

The people were in great agony and torment as the giant-sized monsters unceasingly whipped and drove them into the basement of the castle. There was a gateway to hell, and from the entrance, one could see the light of the flames and hear the frantic sound of torment there. The souls had no strength to escape; they could not even think of it, for their wounds were deep, wide, and hideous. The pain had reached an apex where they felt it no more and, at the same time, had no willpower of their own.

An engraving above the door read, "Abandon All Hope Ye Who Enters." I wondered much at a man who was a little ways from the line that was at the entrance. With many deep wounds all over his body, he lay on the wet stony ground (*it was cold and raining*). His cry was horrendous, and he had no chains hooked unto him (*he was free*), but even though he knew of the looming hell-fires, the desire or will to leave that place was gone from him.

I also saw chains from within the old castle, leading straight into many churches, and some of the believers (*while in service*) were bound to those by means of the flesh hooks.

The state of affairs was this: as soon as some Christians left the presence of God, the creatures dragged the chains with whoever was attached thereto, immediately to the place of torment, and again, we see that the chains are linked to peoples' habits of sin. While in church, they feel free, until afterward they fall in a constant state of torment and thither the gates of hell.

A caution is given here: "Be careful not to walk through the church doors straight to hell."

Now, the human bodies in the line were unable to feel pain, for it had gotten familiar to the hooks and the weight of the chain. The soul, which is the seat of the emotions, passions, and desires, was in constant agony, for it was truly conscious of the present order and the looming conclusion, i.e., the ultimate doom (death) resulting in eternal separation from God.

Let me enlighten you on this: in eternal death, there is no resurrection of the body because of the covering of the first death. It is written in 1 Corinthians 19, "For if the dead rise not, then is not Christ raised: And if Christ be not raised, your faith *is* vain; ye are yet in your sins. Then they also which are fallen asleep in Christ are perished. If in this life only we have hope in Christ, we are of all men most miserable."

"Then *cometh* the end, when he (Jesus) shall have delivered up the kingdom to God, even the Father; when he shall have put down all rule and all authority and power. For he must reign, until he hath put all enemies under his feet" (1 Cor. 15:24-25).

The last enemy *to* be destroyed *is* death, and everyone fears death. *First death is when the body goes in the grave and the second death is eternal separation from God.* This happens after the great judgment day of the living and the dead. "But now is Christ risen from the dead, *and* become the first fruits of them that slept. For since by man *came* death, by man *came* also the resurrection of the dead. For as in Adam all die, even so in Christ shall all be made alive. But every man in his own order: Christ the first fruits; afterward they that are Christ's at his coming" (1 Cor. 15:20-23).

Please observe that the living have a striking propensity for questions that give the stimulus to hope. Hope that is in the believer came from Jesus who gives us the will to go on and seek answers, for we are "not coming, but going" (i.e., we already exist).

Yet there is an insatiable innate desire to know the purpose of life, as in why, how, and what then. However, when the transition (death) is being made from this life to the next, then, and only then, shall all questions be answered, for man will have arrived at his destiny. In Eternity, all things are apparent.

Nevertheless, for the believer on this side of life, Jesus is the answer. He said that He is the way, the truth, and the life. Please note this: the choice that you make in the time given to you by the Creator God will determine your destiny. Moses said to the children of Israel, "I call heaven and earth to record this day against you, that I have set before you life and death, blessing and cursing: therefore choose life, that both thou and thy seed may live;

"That thou mayest love the LORD thy God, and that thou mayest obey his voice, and that thou mayest cleave unto him: for he is thy life, and the length of thy days: that thou mayest dwell in the land which the LORD swore unto thy fathers, to Abraham, to Isaac, and to Jacob, to give them" (Deut. 30:19-20).

> **The following article appeared in the well-respected Finland newspaper, *Ammenusastia***
>
> *"As a communist I don't believe in heaven or the Bible but as a scientist I now believe in hell,"* said Dr. Azzacove. *"Needless to say we were shocked to make such a discovery. But we know what we saw and we know what we heard. And we are absolutely convinced that we drilled through the gates of hell!"*
>
> Dr. Azzacove continued, *". . . the drill suddenly began to rotate wildly, indicating that we had reached a large empty pocket or cavern. Temperature sensors showed a dramatic increase in heat to 2,000 degrees Fahrenheit."*
>
> *"We lowered a microphone, designed to detect the sounds of plate movements down the shaft. But instead of plate movements we heard a human voice screaming in pain! At first we thought the sound was coming from our own equipment."*
>
> *"But when we made adjustments our worst suspicions were confirmed. The screams weren't those of a single human, they were the screams of millions of humans!"*

Actual recording of the sounds can be heard in the article, "The Truth About Hell" by Terry Watkins.

Fourteen

A Look into Hell

Dr. Maurice S. Rawlings, MD, cardiologist and professor of medicine at the University of Tennessee College of Medicine in Chattanooga, was a devout atheist who considered all religion "hocus-pocus." To him, death was nothing more than a painless extinction.

But in 1977, Rawlings was resuscitating a man who came back from the edge of death. The man was terrified and screaming. Rawlings wrote thus: *Each time he regained heartbeat and respiration, the patient screamed, "I am in hell!" He was terrified and pleaded with me to help him. I was scared to death . . . Then I noticed a genuinely alarmed look on his face. He had a terrified look worse than the expression seen in death! This patient had a grotesque grimace, expressing sheer horror! His pupils were dilated, and he was perspiring and trembling—he looked as if his hair was on end.*

There are many stories of near-death experiences in which people report moving down a peaceful tunnel toward a gentle light, but Dr. Rawlings's research, which appeared in *Omni* magazine, demonstrated that about 50 percent of near-death victims report seeing lakes of fire, Devil-like figures, and other sights reflecting the darkness of hell.

"Just listening to these patients has changed my whole life," claims Dr. Rawlings. "There is a life after death, and if I don't know where I'm going, it's not safe to die." Through these experiences, Dr. Rawlings began studying what the Bible had to say about hell and other subjects, and he became a Christian. Two of his books are *Beyond Death's Door* and *To Hell and Back*.

The revelation is this, there are two sorts of hell. I was in prayer in the upper room of my church, when the Lord took my spirit to a place where I saw many people, male and female, moving about. There were no buildings, trees, water, animals, birds, or creeping things in view. Just people walking in circles, crying and mourning, while looking for loved ones or acquaintances but could find none. Among them were heavy-duty machines operating by themselves, clearing the grounds and making room to facilitate more souls.

The sun was not in the sky, but there was light, no night, and very hot, with no place to hide from the heat. In that place of torment, I saw a lady pastor whom I knew very well. She was quite bewildered and sad to discover that she was in such a place. "In my lifetime, I thought I was a good pastor," she said.

We walked to a spot of ground where she revealed to me that it was prepared for her husband. So she earnestly asked me to tell him (*he was a deacon in another church*)) not to go there. The Bible records that "Hell from beneath is moved for thee to meet *thee* at thy coming: it stirreth up the dead for thee, *even* all the chief ones of the earth; it hath raised up from their thrones all the kings of the nations" (Isa. 14:9).

I remember the scripture where Jesus said, "Many will say to me in that day, Lord, Lord, have we not prophesied in thy name? And in thy name have cast out devils? And in thy name done many wonderful works? And then will I profess unto them, I never knew you: depart from me, ye that work iniquity" (Matt. 7:22-23).

The first hell where I met the pastor had light, and it is for those that lived religiously (*or live a so-called good life*). Some say they professed Christ, meaning that they knew the truth at one time but did not obey. The pastor in her lifetime did badly while in her pastorate, and the place where she now stays is situated far away from all life.

Everyone who enters will have no chance of escape, for unwittingly, he or she will have made this choice while living as a mortal. There they must wait for the final judgment.

Fifteen

Death and Undying Penalty

Grave, *sheol.* The grave, the abode of the dead, the netherworld, hell. This noun occurs sixty-five times; its use is broad enough to include the visible grave that houses a dead body and the abyss, that unseen world to which the soul departs in death. The meaning of "grave" is seen in Genesis 37:35; 42:38 and 1 Kings 2:6. *Sheol* speaks of the realm of departed souls in such verses as Psalm 9:17; 16:10; 55:15; 139:8, Isaiah 14:9-11, and Ezekiel 31:15-17; 32:21. The assumed root of *sheol* is *sh'al,* meaning, "to ask, demand, require." Thus, "hell" is a hungry, greedy devourer of humanity, is never full or satisfied, but is always asking for more (see Prov. 27:20). God's promise in Hosea 13:14 is that He will save His people from the power of *sheol* and that He will actually destroy *sheol* in the end.

History of Hell

The Bible is clear that hell was not preexistent, it has not always been. It is apparent that, at some point, hell had to be created as a place of judgment. Furthermore, Revelation 20:14 tells us that hell has an end; it will be cast into the lake of fire. Therefore, since hell has a beginning and an end, we can say it has a history. What do the following verses tell us about hell?

"Therefore hell hath enlarged herself, and opened her mouth without measure: and their glory, and their multitude, and their pomp, and he that rejoices, shall descend into it. And the mean man shall be brought down, and the mighty man shall be humbled, and the eyes of the lofty shall be humbled"

(Isa. 5:14-15). Then shall he say also unto them on the left hand, Depart from me, ye cursed, into everlasting fire, prepared for the devil and his angels" (Matt. 25:41).

We have here a variety of facts about hell: (1) it was made for the Devil, not for humans, (2) it has gotten larger, (3) since Jesus's resurrection, He has held the keys to death and hell.

These facts must all be considered in determining the history of hell. Another key passage that must be considered is Luke 16:19-31. Some scholars suggest that this passage is a parable, while others believe that Jesus was describing an actual occurrence. In either case, there is no question that much conclusive information is given us regarding the place of the dead prior to Jesus's death and resurrection.

Two Biblical Descriptions of Hell

One is of a burning fire. Jesus often used the word *Gehenna* to describe hell. Gehenna was the refuse dump outside Jerusalem that was always on fire. Jesus said hell was a place of worms, maggots, fire, and trouble. From that, we get the image of a lake of fire and the concept of perpetual burning. The evil ones there are full of remorse and torment (Mark 9:43-48).

Jesus also said that hell would be outer darkness, weeping and gnashing of teeth (Matt. 8:12). Here the image is one of terrible loneliness: separation from God and man. Those who are consigned to hell will be put into the inky blackness of eternity, with nobody to turn to or talk to, constantly alone. They will suffer the remorse of knowing they had the opportunity to come into Heaven with God but turned it down.

The Bible speaks of a lake of fire reserved for the Devil and his angels (Matt. 25:41). Human beings were never intended to go into hell. But the ones who choose to reject God will one day follow Satan right into this eternal torment.

There will be no exit from hell, no way out, no second chance. That is why it is so important in this life to receive the pardon that God extends to all men through the Cross of Jesus Christ (Rev. 20:11-15).

According to the descriptions in the Old Testament, Sheol is located in the underworld.

In order to get there, one must descend (Num. 16:30, 33, Job 17:16; 21:13, and Prov. 5:5; 9:18) and one must dig toward it (Amos 9:2). In order to get out, a person would need to ascend (Ps. 30:3). Sheol is located opposite of Heaven (Ps. 139:8; Amos 9:2). It is infested with worms and maggots (Isa. 14:11). This language could be figurative.

The Afterlife in Second Temple Period Literature

In the second temple period (16 BC-AD 70), Jewish writers views on hell were likely shaped by foreign ideas about the afterlife. Persian and Hellenistic ideas of retribution after death may have encouraged a Jewish belief in different fates for the righteous and the godless. For example, in 1 En. 22:8-13, the author describes a divided dwelling for the dead, a sphere for sinners and another sphere for the righteous.

The author of the book of 1Enoch does not seem to distinguish between Sheol and Gehenna—the terms are used interchangeably (1 En. 51:1-3).

Sheol also began to be viewed as an intermediate holding place for the dead, prior to resurrection.

In Iranian thought, the dead had to pass over the Chinvat Bridge in order to reach paradise; demons lurked below the bridge and caused sinners to fall into a pit of torment (Russell, *The Devil*, 255). The book of *2 Esdras* discusses these dual destinies (2 Esd. 7:36). The righteous alone will experience resurrection, according to 1 Enoch (1 En. 22:12-13; 51:1-3). Since resurrection from the dead was only for the righteous, Sheol began to be considered a place of fiery punishment solely for the wicked.

New Testament

The New Testament often distinguishes between (*hadēs*) and (*geenna*). For instance, a few passages simply use (*hadēs*) as a synonym for the death or the grave. For example, Acts 2:27 and 2:31 state that Jesus was not left in (*hadēs*) or "the grave."

The term (*geenna*) occurs ten times in the Gospels (Matt. 5:22, 29; 10:28; 18:9; 23:15, 33; Mark 9:43, 45, 47; Luke 12:5) and also in James 3:6. The word (*hadēs*) occurs nine times in the New Testament (Matt. 11:23; Luke 10:15; 16:23; Acts 2:27, 31; Rev. 1:18; 6:8; 20:13, 14).

Jesus's Teaching on Hell

Jesus teaches that after their death, people either enter the kingdom of God or are cast into (*geenna*) (Matt. 10:28; Luke 13:28). In addition, Jesus discusses three aspects of hell in his teaching: its inhabitants, its features, and the extent of its punishment.

Hell's Inhabitants. Jesus frequently describes those who are destined for (*hadēs*). Jesus tells the inhabitants of Capernaum that their unbelief will lead them to (*hadēs*) (Matt. 11:20-24). Jesus also warns of several sins that might condemn one to (*hadēs*), including calling a spiritual brother or sister a fool

(Matt. 5:22) and giving into sinful tendencies (Matt. 5:29-30). For Jesus, a person is either a child of (*hadēs*) or a child of Abraham (Matt. 23:15; Luke 19:9). Jesus questioned the scribes, Pharisees, and hypocrites about how they expected to escape the condemnation of (*hadēs*) if they kept committing the sins of their ancestors (Matt. 23:31-33). In His preaching, Jesus promised that the gates of (*hadēs*) should not prevail against the church (Matt. 16:18).

Descriptions of Hell. Jesus describes hell as an eternal fire where the Devil and his angels are destined (Matt. 25:41). He also calls it the abyss (Luke 8:31). It is a place of darkness, where a person experiences weeping and gnashing of teeth (Matt. 8:8-12). The weeping suggests suffering and pain, while the gnashing of teeth suggests despair and anger.

Beyond these images, Jesus also portrays hell (*hadēs*) in the parable of the Rich Man and Lazarus (Luke 16:19-31). In this passage, (*hadēs*) is depicted as a permanent abode and a place of torment. Further, it seems it accommodates some individuals, but not others. The rich man went there after dying, and Lazarus did not. Instead, Lazarus was in Abraham's bosom, a traditional designation for the place of the dead who were righteous in life. This parable also teaches about the irreversible nature of punishment in the afterlife.

The Duration of Hell's Punishment

There are two primary perspectives on the extent of hell's punishment. One view contends that the wicked experience eternal conscious suffering ("The Literal"). The other view argues that the wicked are eventually consumed by hell's fire, thereby forfeiting their existence (Fudge, "The Final End").

Matthew 10:28 might imply that hell destroys both the body and the soul, making punishment only temporary. However, other texts support the eternal duration of hell's punishment. For example, Jesus, drawing on Isaiah 66:24, speaks of hell as the place where the worm never dies and the fire is never extinguished (Mark 9:48). In Matthew 25:46, it seems that the punishment is forever rather than for a while. Jesus claims that upon death, some people will go to eternal punishment, while others will enter into eternal life.

I experienced the second hell one night just as I had gotten through preaching in a men's revival. At home exhausted, for the Lord had moved in a tremendous way upon me, and at the same time, I was in the process of recuperating from a surgery. I did not kneel to pray, but I hurriedly sat upon the bed to rest my head on one of my hands, and soon after, I fell in a trance.

I saw the entrance of what appeared to be a building, and persons were going in but none came out. The door was made to open from the top inwards, as a trap door, but the people never contemplated, for they entered the place obsessively, as when one returns home to rest after a hard day's work. I cautiously entered, and the door slammed shut. In an instant, there was gross thick darkness, and no person could see his or her hands when held up close to the face. On the spot, I stood alone and afraid. I called aloud for the next person to hear me, but there was no answer. I could not even hear an echo of my voice or of someone else in a distance.

I could neither measure the place nor tell if I was standing on solid ground or even near the entrance from which I had just made only one step. The walls were missing, and it seemed as if I had stepped into another dimension. Of all the people that entered, there was no one to converse with me. In that place was absolute separation from all life. The only time that those who enter will ever see light and other people will be at the judgment seat of Christ, when all shall appear to give an account of their deeds and what they did with Jesus Christ their Lord.

Hell is a condition and a place. I called out to the Lord to let me out, and He did. I arrest the fact that when a person has reached the end of time (I say time because life goes on after death), that person has no control of what happens next.

In scripture, sleep is often used as a metaphor for death (die), and Sheol (*grave, Hades*) is the destiny of all. Hell is the place of everlasting punishment in darkness (*outer, black*), and the burning lake of unquenchable fire is the final outcome for all those who forfeit life (*perish*) by their rejection of God. It is a place of torment and separation (*fix, gulf*).

The abyss *(bottomless)* is the abode of demons. The scriptures say the following:

> "When the waves of death compassed me, the floods of ungodly men made me afraid; the sorrows of hell compassed me about; the snares of death prevented me" (2 Sam. 22:5-6).

> "But he knoweth not that the dead *are* there; *and that* her guests *are* in the depths of hell" (Prov. 9:18).

> "But I say unto you, that whosoever is angry with his brother without a cause shall be in danger of the judgment.

> "Whosoever shall say to his brother, 'thou fool', shall be in danger of hell fire" (Matt. 5:22).

"And if thine eye offends thee, pluck it out, and cast *it* from thee: it is better for thee to enter into life with one eye, rather than having two eyes to be cast into hell fire" (Matt. 18:9).

"And if thy hand offend thee, cut it off: it is better for thee to enter into life maimed, than having two hands to go into hell, into the fire that never shall be quenched: Where their worm dieth not, and the fire is not quenched" (Mark 9:43-44).

As was said before, all questions are answered in the afterlife, and it is so that the memory is incredibly vivid as it recalls everything in its minutest details about the life lived. In this state, all the senses are heightened, and the feelings become acute. It becomes a woeful (*mournful*) condition (*grief and distress resulting from the serious affliction*), and demise is consciously apprehended. The soul will be subjected to an extreme rigorous awakening.

My meaning is this: while we are living in this body of senses and awareness, there are questions and plans that encompass us immensely. And the essence of love, joy, peace, and sorrow is not conscientiously experienced. For man is limited; he has a boundary that he cannot pass: he cannot have too much of a good or bad thing, for it would kill him. Hence the term "stress." His body has been designed to undertake things proportionately. In the place and state called hell, all boundaries are removed, and as a result, he or she will, without limit, undergo the penalty of actions agonizingly.

The fires of hell depict the torture that the soul will experience while waiting for the judgment. Remorse, the merciless Sheriff, will arrest the mind with charges of, memories of the call to salvation, time wasted, and questions of "why I did not give my heart to God when I had the chance." Finally, the soul enunciates its hopeless doom, and the cycle repeats itself as a person who has lost his mind.

"Behold, I show you a mystery; We shall not all sleep, but we shall all be changed, In a moment, in the twinkling of an eye, at the last trump: for the trumpet shall sound, and the dead shall be raised incorruptible, and we shall be changed. For this corruptible must put on incorruption, and this mortal must put on immortality. So when this corruptible shall have put on incorruption, and this mortal shall have put on immortality, then shall be brought to pass the saying that is written, Death is swallowed up in victory.

"And death and hell were cast into the lake of fire. This is the second death. And whosoever was not found written in the book of life was cast into the lake of fire" (Rev. 20:13-14).

As the war between the Kingdom of darkness and the Kingdom of Light persists, demons oppress humanity, eliciting them to sin against God, making Him angry:

God was moved to destroy that whole nation, as he did in the time of Noah. And Satan was also hoping to contaminate the whole human race, for he hounded for the one that would bruise his head, but God did not reveal his identity to anyone.

You may ask, "When shall all these things come to pass?" The answer is this: He does things in His time, and the end of time is near, at what time Jesus shall put all things under His feet, and Satan will be defeated. When Jesus died, He descended into hell (*Hades*) where He took the keys of death and hell from the Devil, and from since the first man sinned, Satan claimed the rite to hold departed souls captive in prison (*tartarus/the underworld*) because of their sins.

I foresaw the Lord always before my face, for he is on my right hand, that I should not be moved: Therefore did my heart rejoice, and my tongue was glad; moreover also my flesh shall rest in hope: Because thou wilt not leave my soul in hell, neither wilt thou suffer thine Holy One to see corruption" (Acts 2:24-27).

When I shall bring thee down with them that descend into the pit, with the people of old time, and shall set thee in the low parts of the earth, in places desolate of old, with them that go down to the pit, that thou be not inhabited; and I shall set glory in the land of the living (Ezek. 26:20).

"Wherefore he saith, When he ascended up on high, he led captivity captive, and gave gifts unto men. (Now that he ascended, what is it but that he also descended first into the lower parts of the earth? He that descended is the same also that ascended up far above all heavens, that he might fill all things.)" (Rom. 4:8-10)

It was said that as soon as Jesus gave up the Ghost, Satan had a party down in hell, thinking that Jesus had fallen captive in prison just as any other human being. However, Jesus knew no sin, so Satan could not lay a claim on His soul, but all men that died before the crucifixion, he claimed, but to him, this one called for a celebration, since the mighty Son of God became human and was now dead like all others (so thought the evil one). The saying goes on:

Then came a knock on the door, with commands, saying, "Lift up your heads, O ye gates; and be ye lift up, ye everlasting doors; and the King of glory shall come in. Who *is* this King of glory? The LORD strong and mighty, the LORD mighty in battle. Lift up your heads, O ye gates; even lift *them* up, ye everlasting doors; and the King of glory shall come in." Demons asked, "Who is this King of glory? The LORD of hosts, he *is* the King of glory."

The everlasting doors opened of its own accord, and for the first time since Satan became the ruler of darkness (his domain), light shone, and the glory of the Lord radiated throughout. He took the keys from the Devil. The scripture records, "Jesus, when he had cried again with a loud voice, yielded up the ghost. And, behold, the veil of the temple was rent in twain from the top to the bottom; and the earth did quake, and the rocks rent; And the graves were opened; and many bodies of the saints which slept arose, And came out of the graves after his resurrection, and went into the holy city, and appeared unto many" (Matt. 27:50-53).

Once again, God the Father chose the apostles to carry the torch that lights the way back to Eden and Eternity (garden of delight or pleasure (Gen. 2-3), Garden of God (Ezek. 28:13)).

Remember, God saw that it was good, and He came down to commune with man in the cool of the day. So then the *Eden created is idiosyncratic of the condition of mind that God wants us to be in so that He can have pleasure once again with the works of His hands.*

He said that our bodies are His temple. "Know ye not that ye are the temple of God, and *that* the Spirit of God dwelleth in you? If any man defile the temple of God, him shall God destroy; for the temple of God is holy, which *temple* ye are" (1 Cor. 3:16-17).

"What? know ye not that your body is the temple of the Holy Ghost *which is* in you, which ye have of God, and ye are not your own? For ye are bought with a price: therefore glorify God in your body, and in your spirit, which are God's" (1 Cor. 6:19-20).

Sixteen

The Last God (God of the flesh)

I dreamt that some children and I were traveling on a narrow path to find Heaven. There were a few people traveling, and Benny Hinn also, but they continued a little ways from each other (showing that it is a personal quest). We lighted upon a spot where a couple had a business of making pottery. The place of business was situated in the middle of the traffic of souls that are on their quest for Heaven. We stopped to ask them for directions, but they were engaged in unyielding sexual activities.

It was a strange place for them to be making out, but the store was their bedroom, and the passage went right through it; also, it had no doors or private areas. Everyone who passed through could see them in action. The man was small and skinny, and they were both hundreds of years old. The woman was very large, while her face was like dried prunes. She weighed about 350 pounds, and he weighed about 100 pounds. For sure, you could see the age on their skins.

She sat on him and did not move; he did all the actions. The energy that he had to move her up and down was tremendous. As the children looked on, I wondered at the sight with great amazement; nonetheless, we had to ask them for directions. He stopped, she got off him, and he came to show us the way to Heaven, but before he could finish talking to us, the woman, with her constant woeful cries and insatiable burning desire, vehemently urged him to resume sexual activities with her.

This was a day-to-day hourly act for hundreds of years, and the man had no freedom. The children and I hurried on in the direction they gave us, and to our surprise, we had barely left the shop house of sex, when we saw the archway covering the path that leads to Heaven. It was well lit with many colors of lights flickering, attracting people as they came near. The illuminated archway represents the way of Holiness, widely known as the "Highway to Heaven."

As we left, my mind reflected on the man and his wife and wondered why they were so close to Heaven and yet did not try to enter. Later on, I understood that their occupation in antiquity and sensual pleasures had fashioned them thus. It was tactically placed in such proximity by the Devil so as to entertain travelers, with the purpose of distraction to the point of discouraging all who were on their way to Heaven. They being in the middle of the pathway gave them the advantage. Picture inserts describe both persons of my vision.

I also realized that they were once seekers of Heaven but were later turned into sex slaves by the Master of deception and twisted to be gods of the flesh, which cannot enter the kingdom of Heaven. Therefore, the children of God have conquered every god of this world except the "god of the flesh."

Please note that everything man does is for catering to the flesh. While promoting a healthy body and lifestyle, the commercials are fostering sexual suggestions. Man worships the flesh and does not worship his God.

You and many people may ask, "Where was God, the creator of all things, during all this?" Why is it that He who knows all things (*even before the occurrences*) did not design preemptive measures? Answering the first question: God was there all the time, and you must understand that He never makes mistakes.

It took eons of time for Satan to become the master of evil, lies, pride, and deception. Therefore, man, who has been made a little lower than the angels, was no match for him. For God to use the base things of the earth to confound the wise and prudent, man and his appetite must be subjugated (*under control*).

God and the heavenly hosts subsist in Eternity (infinity), subsequent to which there would be no end to Satan's works of iniquity.

The understanding: God in His omnipotence designed time to cultivate maturity for man and bring into being death for the fallen angels, and now there will be an end to evil and its influences.

Generally, his exertion is to be in opposition to God whenever doable. His workings or ways of doing things differ in most reverence with principles of God in diverse times and dispensational eras. For example, in the early ages beginning, i.e., Genesis, Satan's most important work was to cause the fall of man, take over his control (*remember that God made Adam the keeper of the Garden of Eden*), and try to prevent the seed (the Messiah) that would bruise his head from coming into the world in order to ward off his own defeat.

He is a deceiver: "And no marvel; for Satan himself is transformed into an angel of light. And the great dragon was cast out, that old serpent, called the Devil, and Satan, which deceiveth the whole world: he was cast out into the earth, and his angels were cast out with him And I saw an angel come down from heaven, having the key of the bottomless pit and a great chain in his hand. And he laid hold on the dragon, that old serpent, which is the Devil, and Satan, and bound him a thousand years, And cast him into the bottomless pit, and shut him up, and set a seal upon him, that he should deceive the nations no more, till the thousand years should be fulfilled: and after that he must be loosed a little season.

"And I saw thrones, and they sat upon them, and judgment was given unto them: and I saw the souls of them that were beheaded for the witness of Jesus, and for the word of God, and which had not worshipped the beast, neither his image, neither had received his mark upon their foreheads, or in their hands; and they lived and reigned with Christ a thousand years.

"But the rest of the dead lived not again until the thousand years were finished. This is the first resurrection. Blessed and holy is he that hath part in the first resurrection: on such the second death hath no power, but they shall be priests of God and of Christ, and shall reign with him a thousand years. And when the thousand years are expired, Satan shall be loosed out of his prison,

"And shall go out to deceive the nations which are in the four quarters of the earth, Gog and Magog, to gather them together to battle: the number of whom is as the sand of the sea. And they went up on the breadth of the earth, and compassed the camp of the saints about, and the beloved city: and fire came down from God out of heaven, and devoured them. And the devil that deceived them was cast into the lake of fire and brimstone, where the beast and the false prophet are, and shall be tormented day and night forever and ever" (2 Cor. 11:14; Rev. 12:9; 20:1-10).

The utmost significant work of Satan relating to men today is to imitate the principles of truth and knowledge of God as exposed in scripture, in order to deceive saints. "And no marvel; for Satan himself is transformed into an angel of light. Therefore *it is* no great thing if his ministers also be transformed as the ministers of righteousness; whose end shall be according to their works.

Finally, my brethren, be strong in the Lord, and in the power of his might. Put on the whole armor of God, that ye may be able to stand against the wiles of the devil. For we wrestle not against flesh and blood, but against domains, against supremacies, against the rulers of the darkness of this world, against spiritual wickedness in high *places*. Wherefore take unto you the whole armor of God that you may be able to survive in the evil day, and having done all, to counter.

The children of God are encouraged to verify and examine all system of belief and reasoning in the spiritual domain to see if they are of God or Satan (1 Cor. 2:12-16; Phil. 1:9-10; 1 Thess. 5:21-22). It is certain that every belief and worship, teachings and experiences in the world today, cannot be of God.

The knowledge of the truth is the first essential in warfare against demons and errors. The danger is tremendous when believers accept everything and anything in the area of the supernatural, as being from the Lord.

The fact that the believer is a child of God does not stop the Devil from trying every conceivable way to imitate God. Believers are the individuals Satan concentrates on and wages wars against.

There are definite ways outlined in the Word of God whereby each individual can detect what kind of power is seeking to rule him. However, if one neglects to study the Word, he will fall prey to one of Satan's demons, through lack of knowledge of the Word of God, which is why people perish.

Any idea taught as truth that denies or causes doubt and unbelief concerning whatever doctrines taught in the scripture is from Satan and his demons (1 Tim. 4:1-8). Any religion denying the inspiration of the Bible, the reality of God as a person, the virgin birth and divinity of Christ, His death, burial, and bodily resurrection and manifestation after His resurrection, His ascension, and returning to set up a kingdom in the world forever are of Satan and his demons. The Word of God is tested and proven time after time to be absolute truth. The book of Acts records that there are many infallible proofs that Jesus is alive.

Apostle Paul wrote, "And that he was buried, and that he rose again the third day according to the scriptures: And that he was seen of Cephas, (Simon Peter) then of the twelve: After that, he was seen of above five hundred brethren at once; of whom the greater part remain unto this present, but some are fallen asleep. After that, he was seen of James; then of all the apostles. And last of all he was seen of me also, as of one born out of due time."

Paul persecuted the Christians by committing some to imprisonment and some even to death because he did not believe. Jesus Christ met him while he was on the way to hurt some Christians in Damascus; he had a rude awakening, for he heard the voice of God, and it changed his life. A question is asked here: *Why would Paul risk his life for a myth?*

He was a learned man; it is said that he could be the next Caesar or the next King in Jerusalem, but with all his education and political affiliations, he chose to know Christ. His resume stated, "Though I might also have confidence in the flesh. If any other man thinks that he hath whereof he might trust in the flesh, I more: Circumcised the eighth day, of the stock of Israel, *of* the tribe of Benjamin, an Hebrew of the Hebrews; as touching the law, a Pharisee; Concerning zeal, persecuting the church; touching the righteousness which is in the law, blameless. But what things were gain to me, those I counted loss for Christ.

Yes doubtless, and I count all things *but* loss for the excellency of the knowledge of Christ Jesus my Lord: for whom I have suffered the loss of all things, and do count them *but* dung, that I may win Christ, And be found in him, not having mine own righteousness, which is of the law, but that which is through the faith of Christ, the righteousness which is of God by faith:

"That I may know him, and the power of his resurrection, and the fellowship of his sufferings, being made conformable unto his death; He was the greatest Evangelist of his time."

Seventeen

The Path Back to Eternity

The way to God is rightly called a High Way because He ordained it, and His standards are high. He made promises and makes provisions for fulfillment. In many ways, the Christians' pathway to life parallels the Exodus of the Jews from Egypt. It is segmented in this fashion: promise, obstacles, and provision. God told Moses to lead the people to the land of promise:

1. *The Promise:* "And the LORD said: I have surely seen the oppression of My people *in* Egypt, and have heard their cry because of their taskmasters. So I have come down to deliver them out of the hand of the Egyptians, and to bring them up from that land a good and large land, to a land with milk and honey" (Exod. 3:7, 8).

2. *Obstacles* began with Pharaoh (*type of the Devil*) and Egypt (*type of the world*), but the ultimate difficulties rested within the people of God. Their taskmaster treated them with the utmost contempt. They were not ready to inherit the promise with slave-to-sin mentalities. When they passed through the Red Sea, it was a type of baptism (*born again*) to a new man individually. The new birth is necessary for salvation. They had to be groomed within and without to learn the ultimate lesson of faith in God. The grooming was of such order: They should remember all the ways which the LORD their God led them for forty years in the wasteland, self-effacing them, to ascertain and know what was in their heart, whether they would keep his commandments, or no.

"And he humbled thee, and suffered thee to hunger, and fed thee with manna, which thou knewest not, neither did thy fathers know; that he might make thee know that man doth not live by bread only, but by every *word* that proceedeth out of the mouth of the LORD doth man live. Thy raiment waxed not old upon thee, neither did thy foot swell, these forty years. Thou shalt also consider in thine heart, that, as a man chasteneth his son, *so* the LORD thy God chasteneth thee.

What kind of people could an environment of hatred, pain, starvation, little to no self-esteem, and bound to chains of depravity, with no power to make decisions and idol worshippers, produce after over 400 years?—only people who are poor, weak, helpless, chafed, heartless, faithless, depraved, and unyielding. But God remembered His promise to Abraham. Moses had to lead a people that were not free to worship God in spirit and in truth.

3. *Provision:* The pathway is a coordination of principles and doctrines ordained for man by his Creator and are written on the pages of time, using the lives of Holy Men as the pen, ink, and paper. It is a lifestyle of the highest array or measure. Sadly though, many failed miserably, and a few conquered. "In the way of righteousness *is* life; and *in* the pathway *thereof there is* no death" (Prov. 12:28). The ways of God are higher than our ways.

"Enter ye in at the strait gate: for wide *is* the gate, and broad *is* the way, that leadeth to destruction, and many there be which go in thereat: Because strait *is* the gate, and narrow *is* the way, which leadeth unto life, and few there be that find it" (Matt. 7:13-14).

No other religion has history so froth with love, blood, sweat, tears, wars, and promises that brings the entire world to trepidation (*distress*). Yet Christ kept His promise of bringing man closer to his Creator.

Amidst the many bedlams (chaos caused by man's blatant rejection of God's laws), He graciously prepared this *course* for man to tread, but it would take him a lifetime to finish.

The set course is narrow, treacherous, difficult, painful, and obscure, with many decisions to make but ultimately leads to perfection (*maturity*) and foster a consummate relationship with God as was intended. If he learns to do well and walk in the light of God's Word, then will he be ready to live in Eternity with Him.

All scripture refers not to the Old Testament as a whole, but to every part of the Old Testament and New Testament. Inspiration (Greek *theopneustos*) means "God breathed out" the scriptures, and not that God breathed into the human authors. The authors themselves were controlled by God so that they were not left to their human limitations.

"For the prophecy came not in old time by the will of man: but holy men of God spake *as they were* moved by the Holy Ghost" (2 Pet. 1:21).

The scriptures are not only profitable for salvation, doctrine, reproof, correction, and instruction, but for sanctification and Christian growth as well. They are not only the road map to Heaven, but also the road map of the Christian life. They are all we need for steady progress on the pathway.

When sanctification takes place in the man of God, and he is perfect or mature, the scriptures are designed and appropriated for service, "furnished unto all good works." Doctrine always should emanate in good works.

"Because strait *is* the gate, and narrow *is* the way, which leadeth unto life, and few there be that find it" (Matt. 7:14). These verses have an application to the gospel by depicting the two roads and destinies of the human race. "The wide gate and broad way lead to destruction". The narrow gate and difficult way lead to life. "Jesus is both the gate and the way".

However, while this is a valid application of the passage, the interpretation is for believers. Jesus is saying that to follow Him would require faith, discipline, and endurance, and this difficult life is the only life worth living. If you choose the easy way, you will have plenty of company, but you will miss God's best for you.

We read the life of Jacob, how he had to run away from his home, because his brothers tried to kill him, but the time came when he had to return. And Jacob vowed a vow, saying, "If God will be with me, and keep me on this road that I go, and will give me bread to eat, and a garment to put on, and I come again to my father's house in peace—then shall Jehovah be my God. And this stone, which I have set up *for* a pillar, shall be God's house; and of all that thou wilt give me I will without fail give the tenth to thee."

He did not thrust Adam and his future family out of paradise without any hope of ever returning. He made provision for them to return but as transformed Sons of God, born again through Jesus Christ and His shed blood. To live without hope is wretchedness. Apostle Paul wrote, "If in this life only we had hope we would be men most miserable."

Man cannot rely on his own method of doing things. Solomon also wrote, "There is a way that seems right unto a man but the end thereof are the ways of death." Jesus said that "no good thing dwells in the flesh."

This pathway is the method that God ordained for His children to walk on their way back to Eden and Eternity. "And a highway shall be there, and a way and it shall be called The Way of Holiness; the unclean shall not pass over it; but it *shall be* for those: the wayfaring men, though fools, shall not err *therein*" (Isa. 35:8). It is a lifestyle of faith.

"And when Abram was ninety years old and nine, the LORD appeared to Abram, and said unto him, I *am* the Almighty God; walk before me, and be thou perfect" (Gen. 17:1).

"And the LORD spake unto Aaron, saying, Do not drink wine nor strong drink, thou, nor thy sons with thee, when ye go into the tabernacle of the congregation, lest ye die: *it shall be* a statute for ever throughout your generations: *And that ye may put difference between holy and unholy, and between unclean and clean;* And that ye may teach the children of Israel all the statutes which the LORD hath spoken unto them by the hand of Moses" (Lev. 10:8-11).

The Pathway is Obedience: "Now therefore, if ye will obey my voice indeed, and keep my covenant, then ye shall be a peculiar treasure unto me above all people: for all the earth *is* mine: And ye shall be unto me a kingdom of priests, and an holy nation" (Exod. 19:5-6). "But his delight *is* in the law of the LORD; and in his law doth he meditate day and night" (Ps. 1:2). "But this thing commanded I them, saying, Obey my voice, and I will be your God, and ye shall be my people: and walk ye in all the ways that I have commanded you, that it may be well unto you" (Jer. 7:23).

Integrity:

There was a man from ancient Oz. (*As far as we can gather, "the land of Uz" lay either east or southeast of Palestine, north of the southern Arabians and west of the Euphrates; and, lastly, adjacent to the Edomites of Mount Seir*). Satan hated him, mainly because his lifestyle was not like any ordinary man throughout the regions. He lived to please God and taught his children the same. Satan saw that God favored him, so he tried to accuse him of wrongdoing. The accusation had twofold intent. First to destroy the mortal man's favor and relationship with God, thinking that the seed pronounced to bruise his heel would stem from that man. Secondly, God would not bless a man full of un—righteousness, and the man was like all men of earth. So Satan accused God also of been biased by blessing the man to be the richest of all on the earth for he Satan went back and forth throughout the earth knowing good and evil people. But he was the cause and perpetuator of evil.

The charge of been unjust and in favor of a mortal man (*whom he thought God did not know well enough*), is saying that he Satan was treated unfairly, for he is known by all heavenly beings. And though Satan got permission to trouble the man, he never sinned nor charged God foolishly. His statement of integrity was "My lips shall not speak wickedness, nor my tongue utter deceit. God forbid that I should justify you: till I die I will not remove mine integrity from me. My righteousness I hold fast, and will not let it go: my heart shall not reproach *me* so long as I live" (Job 27:4-6)

It Is the Way of Faith and Trust:

God consigned a statement within the patriarch Jacob, a fixed rule when the moment he name was changed to Israel. You see the name Jacob meant supplant. For he tricked his brother twice, and his father-in-law many times to get wealth. By doing so God's hands were tied and the walk of faith came to a halt. It is not of works lest any man should boast. The promise was made to Jacob's grandfather Abraham by God, and must be fulfilled by His way at His timing. However, It is easy for humans to go astray, yet not without enticement from the enemy of souls. Jehovah-Jireh (meaning provider) made provision for his return to the old landmark. He permitted the enemy to stir trouble for Jacob and his family. God graciously appeared changed his name to Israel (father of many nations) and energized his faith for the mission.

If in this life we have hope only, we will be men most miserable. Jacob renewed his faith in the promises of Jehovah, and trusted that He would be kept wherever he went through out his generations.

That the generation to come might know *them*, *even* the children *which* should be born; *who* should arise and declare *them* to their children: That they might set their hope in God, and not forget the works of God, but keep his commandments: And might not be as their fathers, a stubborn and rebellious generation; a generation *that* set not their heart aright, and whose spirit was not steadfast with God" (Ps. 78:5-7).

People that have no faith in God cannot please Him. Queen Esther found favor in the King, so he stretched out the scepter to receive her. God was not about to change His mind and use someone else. No, He keeps promises and whom he foreknew, He called and justified (or prepared) and make ready.

Trust: Trust is an important manner in relationships. If there is no trust, there is no love. In God's dealings with mankind such characteristic is imperative, for it goes hand in hand with faith, without which it is impossible to please Him. Abraham believed God who reckoned to him as righteousness. Righteousness exalts a nation but sin is a reprimand to any people. So trust in the Lord with all your heart, and lean not to your own understanding, but in all your deportments acknowledge Him and he shall direct your path.

It Is a Highway of Truth:

God is faithful to His Word, for He watches over it to perform it. I will accomplish what it was sent to do, and prosper where he pleases. So with this in mind, we must continue in the Word the he spoke especially concerning me. He told Israel "If thy children take heed to their way, to walk before me in truth with all their heart and with all their soul, there shall not fail thee (said he) a man on the throne of Israel" (1 Kings 2:4).

"For the law was given by Moses, *but* grace and truth came by Jesus Christ. No man hath seen God at any time; the only begotten Son, which is in the bosom of the Father, he hath declared *him*" (John 1:17-18).

Eighteen

Face-to-Face with God

While awaiting a day surgery in hospital, God visited me face-to-face. The room was transformed into a regular-size bedroom, and there was neither normal lighting nor any comforts of home, i.e., bed, couch, chairs and so on. The temperature was perfect. It was well lit with His glory; amazingly, there were no shadows or reflections.

The scripture says that "God is the father of light and in Him is no darkness. Do not err, my beloved brethren. Every good gift and every perfect gift is from above, and cometh down from the Father of lights, with whom is no variableness, neither shadow of turning" (James 1:16-17). There is neither darkness nor evil in Him, for He is veracity, i.e., absolute truth. So when He makes promises, they are based upon facts.

"Paul, a servant of God, and an apostle of Jesus Christ, according to the faith of God's elect, and the acknowledging of the truth which is after godliness; In hope of eternal life, which God, *that cannot lie*, promised before the world began; But hath in due times manifested his word through preaching, which is committed unto me according to the commandment of God our Saviour."

Even though the room appeared to be empty, it was fully furnished. We were seated but on nothing physical. This interprets that in the presence of God, things that are made of material substance are unfounded.

Faith was the substance of the furniture, so we sat on faith. I truly experienced what the psalmist wrote: "In His presence there is fullness of joy and at His right hand, there are pleasures forevermore."

To further emphasize on what the meaning of this experience is while we are living in this material world, there are questions that must be answered, such as these: (1) Who am I? (2) What is my purpose? (3) Is there life after death? (4) Is God real, and is there a Devil? These questions keep us on a quest to know the truth that lies beyond the veil.

The soul which is the seat of our emotions, feelings, passions, and desires is in constant need of pacification, i.e., it cannot be completely satisfied. The Spirit is the seat of the intellect and will. With this, we make decisions, plans, and choices. The Body houses them. Apostle Paul wrote, "But I am carnal, sold under sin.

Now because of the "sin principle", there is a constant confusion likened unto a war within each man of sin. The war and wrestling match is on this wise, what one does is not what he permits but what he hates to do that he finds himself doing, hence repetitious actions of wrongdoing. One comes to realize through the Spirit of Grace from God that in mankind that is full of sin dwells no good thing. The only solution is destruction or death. The wages of sin is death but God's gift is eternal life. But how could one dies and yet live? For suicide is not lawful. The Word of God states that, been buried with Christ in baptism, will result in resurrection to a new life, even as he died and was buried, and rose from the grave. Only in the Son we have life. So we must crucify the deeds of the carnal man by through repentance with sincere desire to forsake them, in order to win the battle of life.

For I delight in the law of God after the inward man: But I see another law in my members, warring against the law of my mind, and bringing me into captivity to the law of sin which is in my members. O wretched man that I am! who shall deliver me from the body of this death? I thank God through Jesus Christ our Lord. So then with the mind I myself serve the law of God; but with the flesh the law of sin.

This tells of the elusiveness (*hard to find*) of humanity in cognition (*spiritual knowledge and reasoning*). He is plagued with indecision, for he was made a creature subjected unto vanity (*futility*).

Let us also look at a baby in the womb. It has no cares or plans nor questions or desires and does not worry about the five senses of the body, for in that sack, all is provided. If the mother stresses out for whatever the reason(s), it will affect the child.

Therefore, she must take all necessary precaution to ensure a safe delivery. Now, at birth, the child takes its first breath, and if it does not cry on its own, the doctor may give it a slap (*stillbirth signifies death*). Then it will cry because of pain, loneliness, needs, and dependencies.

The soul of man experiences sentiments during a lifetime, just like the newborn babe but in fewer proclivities (*natural tendency*), for the reason of age, experience, and maturity. The scripture says, "If in this life only we have hope, we would be men most miserable."

Job also wrote that "Man that is born of a woman is of a few days, and they are full of trouble." Being alive in this world without Christ is as the French say, "Le Miserable."

In God's presence, I felt like the child in the womb, and in addition, His voice was calm, sweet and assuring, full of hope, safe, and very satisfying. His voice to me makes the difference; when He speaks, it relieves my troubled mind. It is the only voice I hear that makes the difference, and I will follow one day at a time. Often, when I remember the sound of His voice, tears come to my eyes.

The air and room were pure, with no dust or familiar odors (*not even of fresh air*). You see, if a millionth particle of earth is in a glass of water, you might not be able to see it with your naked eyes. Now consider being able to see your entire world around you, with eyes of only 100 time zoom lens of a magnifying glass. I am sure that you would have an instant awakening to things hidden. My soul felt at home as if I went back into my mother's womb. I had arrived and did not care to leave, for my soul could not feel the chill of loneliness or the vise grip of discouragement nor did I remember how pain felt.

My soul was incredibly cognizant (aware) because I had no more questions, for I had found the answer, and all things were apparent. God waited until I had been acquainted with His presence; then He said to me, "Ask me all the questions that you have." So I asked why the pain, why I was not healed, and when it will stop. He told me that I had to die as Jesus died in order to live, and to know pain is to be acquainted with compassion, and it is compassion that heals and delivers, for that is how Jesus healed the sick and saved the sinner.

The pain positioned me for a higher dimension in God, where miracles with signs and wonders happen. Jesus was crucified on the cross and transformed from Son of Man to be the King of kings. God continued to say to me, "When the pain stops, you will be unhappy," the reason being there are many, many souls to be healed, delivered, and saved (*as a reward*). Each moment of pain represented a soul healed and saved from sin, sickness, and disease. So I said, "OK, Lord, your will be done in my life." I asked Him many more questions until there was none left.

Afterward, He took me on a tour of the city; there I experienced the immense difference of purity, holiness, and uncleanness. It was quite appalling to discover that the world I live in is extremely mucky. Wherever I looked, there were puddles or pools of human internal waste.

The voices of adults and children were atrocious and depicted the sound of liquid excreta exiting the body (*bowel movement*).

Because of this, their prayers could not be heard. Looking on man through the eyes of God, I saw the abomination of the mind. I fully grasped what Jesus said: "It's not what goes into a man that defiles him, but it is what comes out."

The tour went on into His house (the Church), where I saw a pastor with three wives, all three attending the same church, while another minister had continuous fights with his wife each week before they went to preach. Those wars persistently drained him, for he was busy trying to keep his wife in check and, as a result, could not find time to fast and pray or even read his Bible to receive a message from God for his congregation. Therefore, he gathered some old bones with whatever leftover food he found (spiritual food) from years ago and served his church.

The scenes of corruption went on and on, and still, there was no clean place found for God to stand. Naturally, I was very sad, for I felt the love of the Father for His children.

Reflecting on Psalm 14:2-3, "The LORD looked down from heaven upon the children of men, to see if there were any that did understand, *and* seek God. They are all gone aside, they are *all* together become filthy, there *is* none that doeth good, no, not one. Nevertheless, He led captivity, captives and gave gifts to men. He makes His ministers flaming swords of fire."

God is equipping the body of Christ with authority. As I was broken in spirit, a massive sense of purpose came upon me. God wants His people to be saved, and I must follow the great commission given by Jesus in Matthew 28:19: "Go Ye Therefore."

Nineteen

Back to Eternity

When Christ died, He took away the flaming sword from the entrance of the garden, leaving it free for those who have received Him as Lord and Savior and are washed in His blood, to enter and eat of the tree of life freely. He has broken down the middle wall of partition and gave entrance into the most Holy Place (*the presence of God*), for the father was pleased with His sacrifice, and it pleases Him to see the shed blood of His Son Jesus painted on the door lintels of our hearts.

Today, the Father is raising an army that will take the kingdom by force: "And from the days of John the Baptist until now the kingdom of heaven suffereth violence, and the violent take it by force. For all the prophets and the law prophesied until John" (Matt. 11:12-13).

Joel prophesied saying that in the last days, God will pour out His spirit upon all flesh. "But this is that which was spoken by the prophet Joel; And it shall come to pass in the last days, saith God, I will pour out of my Spirit upon all flesh: and your sons and your daughters shall prophesy, and your young men shall see visions, and your old men shall dream dreams: And on my servants and on my handmaidens I will pour out in those days of my Spirit; and they shall prophesy" (Acts 2:17-18).

And still yet, the devil is angry with God and misery to the natives of the world; for the devil has gone mad having great wrath for he knows that he only has a short while till Jesus returns, Maranatha.

In frustration, he tried to destroy the truth by killing the Apostles. However longer the persecution; grander the spreading of the Gospel.

The time has come for the sons of God to arise with the fire of the Holy Ghost and proclaim liberty, for salvation has come to man.

Which is greater—Origin or Destiny? Some say that Origin is greater, for without a beginning, there can be no end. I say that the Origin of a thing is greater than its Destiny because that thing was made a subject matter. According to demands, a watch was made for time, a chair to sit on, a bed to lie on, a glass to drink from and so on. Therefore, the Origin of a thing is greater.

The Origin of man is not greater than his Destiny, for he came from God and will return to Him, but the choice that he makes could have a profound effect on making his Origin greater. Man is given time to acquire perfection, a necessary trait to portray, in order to live in the presence of God who rules Eternity. Eternity is man's Destiny. Therefore, in terms of man, neither Origin nor Destiny is greater if he obeys God and keeps His laws. Sadly though, the sinner's Origin is greater.

It is appointed unto man once to die, and after that comes the judgment. Jesus said, "I go to prepare a place for you that where I am, there you may be also." He lived in a house of mortality for thirty-three and a half years and then went back to where He came.

Eternity is a timelessness condition, quality, or fact of being without a beginning or end. Time is a dimension that enables two identical events occurring at the same point in space to be distinguished, measured by the interval between the events.

Where was any man when God laid the foundations of the earth? Did anyone take a survey for Him? What holds the world in place, or who put the stars in place? Who cause the sea to remain where lies so that it cannot cover the dry land?

Neither you nor I can fathom eternal life. "For God so loved the world that He gave His only begotten Son, that whosoever believeth in Him, should not perish but have eternal life" (John 3:16). This is the golden text of the Bible. Eternal life is the destiny of all who choose to follow Jesus Christ who is the Way, the Truth, and the Life.

Some people will not to receive Him as their Lord and Savior because they do not believe they have an immortal soul. Solomon, the wisest man that ever lived, wrote in Ecclesiastes, Chapter 12, "The body goes to the grave and the spirit goes back to God who gave it." I am certain that his wisdom and experiences were never questioned nor rejected by history. Even though he was a backslidden preacher, he took the time to impart wisdom to his young men. Everyone today believes history and that it never lies. If history is a lie, then all experiences are fables.

Let us now turn to further emphasis of truths and realities that are written in the Word of God. Man's composition is of Body, Soul, and Spirit. The soul is the seat of the emotions, passions, desires, and feelings. The spirit is the seat of the intellect and will, i.e., processes of conclusion or determination manufactured. The body is the house of both, through which sentiments are experienced. The body will go back to the earth, for it was made of it, and the soul and spirit are eternal and must be housed.

Our Creator God wisely constructed the plan that a new body be prepared for the blood-washed saints and one of a different order for the sinners and ungodly. Therefore, if we have no soul, then we would be just like the animals in this world, existing by instinctive biological drive, i.e., an inborn pattern of behavior characteristic of a species and shaped by biological necessities, such as survival and reproduction, but not with purpose and destiny. Man has the power to choose. Creatures in the lower order do not have this power, for they are driven by instinct. Man was given responsibility to take dominion over creation. He was also given the power of speech and the ability to create. If not, all wisdom and understanding are lost, and this is futility and vexation of spirit.

We must conclude that he has a future beyond the grave, and time is given to him to acquire knowledge, wisdom, and understanding in order to worship and serve His Creator who lives in Eternity. Such is the hope of humanity. Jesus went to make ready this place and condition for weary souls to rest. He said it, "I go to prepare a place for you." However, with His life, He made vivid the path back to where the sons of God fell from grace, but there is a war going on in the members of man. For the spirit lusts against the flesh, and the flesh wars against the spirit, bringing about contrariness and making him wretched.

Back then, Abraham knew of the city and so he traveled looking for it. The apostles knew of it and would not turn back for all the riches and fame or torture in the world. Therefore, they became martyrs, choosing to suffer for their faith. Heaven is not a condition or a situation as many would conclude, but rather it is a place with conditions.

But now we desire and hope for a better *motherland*, that is, a heavenly, but God prepared one for all who receive Jesus Christ as Lord and Savior. Described in Revelation

"And God shall wipe away all tears from their eyes; and there shall be no more death, neither sorrow, nor crying, neither shall there be any more pain: for the former things are passed away.

"He that overcometh shall inherit all things; and I will be his God, and he shall be my son. But the fearful, and unbelieving, and the abominable, and murderers, and whoremongers, and sorcerers, and idolaters, and all liars, shall have their part in the lake which burneth with fire and brimstone: which is the second death. And there came unto me one of the seven angels which had the seven vials full of the seven last plagues, and talked with me, saying, Come hither, I will shew thee the bride, the Lamb's wife.

"And showed me that great city, the holy Jerusalem, descending out of heaven from God, Having the glory of God: and her light *was* like unto a stone most precious, even like a jasper stone, clear as crystal; And had a wall great and high, *and* had twelve gates, and at the gates twelve angels, and names written thereon, which are *the names* of the twelve tribes of the children of Israel: On the east three gates; on the north three gates; on the south three gates; and on the west three gates.

"And the wall of the city had twelve foundations, and in them the names of the twelve apostles of the Lamb. And he that talked with me had a golden reed to measure the city, and the gates thereof, and the wall thereof. And the city lies foursquare, and the length is as large as the breadth: and he measured the city with the reed, twelve thousand furlongs. The length and the breadth and the height of it are equal. And he measured the wall thereof, an hundred *and* forty *and* four cubits, *according to* the measure of a man, that is, of the angel.

"And the building of the wall of it was *of* jasper: and the city *was* pure gold, like unto clear glass. And the foundations of the wall of the city *were* garnished with all manner of precious stones. The first foundation *was* jasper; the second, sapphire; the third, a chalcedony; the fourth, an emerald; The fifth, sardonyx; the sixth, sardius; the seventh, chrysolite; the eighth, beryl; the ninth, a topaz; the tenth, a chrysoprasus; the eleventh, a jacinth; the twelfth, an amethyst.

"And the twelve gates *were* twelve pearls; every several gate was of one pearl: and the street of the city *was* pure gold, as it were transparent glass. And I saw no temple therein: for the Lord God Almighty and the Lamb are the temple of it. And the city had no need of the sun, neither of the moon, to shine in it: for the glory of God did lighten it, and the Lamb *is* the light thereof. And the nations of them which are saved shall walk in the light of it: and the kings of the earth do bring their glory and honour into it. And the gates of it shall not be shut at all by day: for there shall be no night there.

Now this I say, brethren, that mortal man cannot receive the kingdom of God; neither doth perversion receive purity.

According to these scriptures, man must be changed or born again to re enter Eternity. Charles Darwin had a vision of an inevitable change, but the vision was thwarted by the Devil to attribute it to the evolutional theory.

However, life is a consummation of changes, and there is yet one change pending, and the whole creation awaits:

You may not fully understand the reality in what was said. Let me explain. While in time, we live by fixed laws and rules that make us dependent. We are to procreate and cultivate knowledge, understanding, and wisdom. We are in constant need of replenishing the body, for it needs sustenance, or it will die. From the day that Adam was cursed, death took control. So man must till and subdue the earth in order to survive, and needs must be met.

The seven sayings of Christ on the Cross embody these needs: (1) My God, My God, why hast thou forsaken me? Tell of spiritual needs of acceptance (belonging to, identify), (2) Father, forgive them—psychological needs, (3) Today thou shalt be with me in paradise—acceptance needs, (4) Into thy hands I commend my Spirit—safety needs, (5) Woman, behold thy son. Son, behold thy mother—love needs (6) I thirst—physiological (body) needs, (7) It is finished—self-actualization needs, i.e., awareness with a purpose, answering the questions: Why was I made? What am I? Where am I headed? And such characterize the fundamental nature of humanity.

"Man shall not live by bread alone, said Jesus, but by every word that proceeds out of the mouth of God do man live." Now if the Word of God is forever, then this statement tells me that man was made to live forever.

And in order for him to live, he must consume the Word of God together with the natural food.

Remember the manna that perished after only a day? Some was kept in a pot for a memorial for hundreds of years. The manna was angels' food, and it typified the Word of God that man shall live by. Now what will happen to the part of man that is eternal? Is it left to drift away into oblivion? God would not nurture and leave it to perish, for His Word is eternal, and His Word is, therefore, man's food for eternal life (we are what we eat); this is his destiny. However, it is sad to know that some will go to happiness and others to absolute contempt and punishment.

Now everyone that has this hope purifies himself from the filth of this world. How is this done? So take heed to the word of God, and obey his commandments daily. Give serious attention to a warning or advice and take into account when acting. One cannot ignore the signs and expect to get by. Such individual is heading for a great dilemma.

One need not do anything to go to hell. Just doing nothing will get you there. How can you say that, preacher? Well, we all were born in sin and shaped in iniquity; this is the core of our nature. We cannot produce righteousness.

God said that all our good deeds in his sight (*doing what seems right*) is as filthy rags before him." Therefore, in order to enter the kingdom of Heaven, we must be born again, meaning, a whole new lifestyle that is led by the Holy Spirit. His words have I hid in my heart that I may not sin against him.

The Word is similar to seeds that must be cultivated, while some are hid for future planting. It must be tended with care, for it is our sustenance and the staff of life. Without it, life will be short-lived, with no hope of living. Man will be without excuse if he stays in sin.

God has clearly marked the pathway back to Eternity, by way of His Son Jesus Christ, who shed His blood on the cross for the remission of sins. He boldly and plainly declared, "I am the way, the truth, and the life: no man cometh unto the Father, but by me" (John 14:6). Jesus proved to us that we could live in hell and still make it to Heaven. The standards set forth whereby we have access to Heaven are very high. He is acquainted with our weaknesses and will not leave us to forage by ourselves.

He left us The Paraclete, (*means first advocate, defender, helper, strengthene*r) which is the Holy Ghost, to stand by for the purpose of teaching and guiding us to the right pathway, leading to our destiny. With Him by our sides, we can make it back.

As was described in statements earlier, Heaven is a magnificent home that Jesus has gone to make ready for those who are born again, not of flesh and blood, but of the Spirit and the Blood of Jesus Christ. There are many obstacles and mountains (spiritually speaking) in our way, but with Jesus, we will climb higher every day. As Heaven is real, so is the lake of fire. Knowing that the Bible is the infallible (*inerrant, incapable of making a mistake*) Word of God, we must realize that the things that are written therein will come to pass.

"The Revelation of Jesus Christ, which God gave unto him, to shew unto his servants things which must shortly come to pass; and he sent and signified *it* by his angel unto his servant John: Who bare record of the word of God, and of the testimony of Jesus Christ, and of all things that he saw. Blessed *is* he that reads, and they that hear the words of this prophecy, and keep those things which are written therein: for the time *is* at hand" (Rev. 1:1-3).

Where will you be, a million years from now, will you be happy; will you be singing? While ages roll throughout eternity. I ask this question, where you will be?

We are now in the last days of our pilgrimage, back to Eternity, and we must be ready, for in an hour when we think not, our Lord will appear. The skies shall unfold, preparing His entrance; the stars shall applaud Him with thunders of praise. The sweet light in His eyes shall; enhance those awaiting and we shall behold Him our Savior and Lord. I ask this question, "Where will you be a million years from now, will you be happy, will you be singing, while ages roll throughout eternity, where will you be?

Many saints were martyrs for the gospel, but because they knew their God is real, they continued unto death and never gave up.

While the true children of God spend eternity with Him, the sinners and the ungodly will spend theirs in the fires of hell. Jesus never used lies to bring out truths. In the book of Luke, the story of the rich man that died and went to hell, Jesus said, "And in *hell* he lift up his eyes, being in torments, and seeth Abraham afar off, and Lazarus in his bosom; a story of a rich man and a poor of which both died, speaks of the reality of that place called hell. The wicked shall be turned into *hell*, and all the nations that forget God" (Ps. 9:17).

Hell, the place of everlasting punishment in darkness (*outer; black*) and burning in a lake of unquenchable fire, is the final outcome for all those who forfeit life (perish) by their rejection of God. It is a place of torment (*gnash, tooth, worm*) and separation (*fix, gulf*). The abyss (*bottomless*) is the abode of demons.

"Today, if you should hear His voice, harden not your heart as in the day of provocation in the wilderness, when they tempted Him and He sent poisonous snakes and killed many of them. Now is the time of salvation. He is nearer than when we first believed."

There is a Heaven to gain and a hell to shun. The day after the rapture of the saints will be the saddest one since the dawn of creation. Just imagine when everywhere you look, people are weeping, confused, and wandering about, for loved ones are missing. That day is not an illusion of our heads. Prophecy never lies but always come to pass.

Twenty

God Cried

Jesus wept (John 11:35). In another vision from God, I saw the sun shrunk to a smaller size and (*like in a movie*) entered the house where some people and I were attending a function. Some were terrified, while others screamed. Bravely, I walked up close to where it rested, and it was hot. As I got closer, I saw what looked like a doorway and therein were people that lived on earth from the beginning of time till present, sped by in a moment (*like a movie on fast-forward*).

I was able to identify Old Testament characters, starting from Adam to Moses, through to the silent years, i.e., between the testaments. Just above in the clouds stood an audience of angelic beings, with the Almighty God Himself. All were dressed in white apparel. The scene was intriguing; therefore, I went to have a closer look, and again, in another moment of time, I saw this present-day generation, beginning from the birth of Jesus Christ all the way through these days, and then God cried.

While crying, He told me that He was pleased with the generations of the past, even though a great number of them sinned and displeased Him greatly, but in this generation, an alarming number of souls will be lost for hell and the lake of fire. He kept on crying. I felt the fathomless burden of love from the heart of the Omnipotent God our Father and could not bear to know that so many people are doomed. I hastily woke out of the vision because the panoramic view caused too much heaviness on my heart.

This view of the passion of His deep apprehension for humankind has changed my life and way of thinking toward souls. I am left with a burden to see people give their hearts to the Lord, be healed, and be saved from their sins. The vision forced me to realize the importance of preaching the gospel, and woe am I if I preach not the gospel of Jesus Christ with urgency. How the Father wants men to go to Heaven!

When Jesus saw how the people wept at the tomb of His friend Lazarus, He wept also, for He was touched by the feelings of their infirmities. He cared for their soul. He called the body to come forth from the grave, and he that was dead and wrapped up came out of the tomb alive. Jesus did this to prove His love for them and that He must be glorified and they could apprehend the love of God.

Cast all your cares on the Lord, for He cares for you. Still, He goes by fixed rules that are carefully set forth in the written word. His words came to us by means of the blood, pain, and suffering of His holy servants and the crucifixion of Jesus Christ, His Son. Every knee shall bow, and every tongue shall confess that Jesus is Lord. I will be looking for you in Eternity.

Many people do not understand the things of God because *they are spiritually discerned*. Apostle Paul wrote, "And without controversy great is the mystery of godliness: God was manifest in the flesh, justified in the Spirit, seen of angels, preached unto the Gentiles, believed on in the world, received up into glory" (1 Tim. 3:13).

It is appointed unto man once to die, and after death comes the judgment, and this standing appointment provides evidence that there is life after death and that he must return to whence he came. He said, "So shall my word be that goes forth out of my mouth: it shall not return unto me void, but it shall accomplish that which I please, and it shall prosper *in the thing whereto I sent it*" (Isa. 55:11b).

Of the millions of people, from past to present, that have trusted in Him and His Word, none has returned to invalidate. Still, if there were one, such would stand alone, and the odds would be awe-inspiring. We occupy a body of senses and feelings with a mind that must be enlightened by inquisition as to what is purpose and the why's, where's and how's pertaining to existence.

Nevertheless, a transformation is prerequisite to destiny subsequently, where all things are apparent. The seeker should take all necessary precaution to **Ask**, **Seek**, and **Knock**, walk in the light of God's Word, and be crucified with Jesus Christ the author and finisher of our faith, in order to fulfill providence.

In the United States write:

Apostle Rudolph A. Whyte
5594 Muirfield Village Circle,
Lake Worth Florida, USA
33463

In Canada write:

Apostle Rudolph A. Whyte
34 Bucksburn Road
Etobicoke Ontario, M9V 3V3
Prayer Lines: 1-803-572—(help) 4357, 1-416-873-9250

Web site: worlddeliveranceministriesinc.org
E-mail: wdminc@hotmail.com
Apostle Whyte is available for crusades, concerts, revivals, seminars, and evangelistic meetings.

NOTES

Dake, F. J. (1999). *The Dake Annotated Reference Bible and Commentary.* Lawrenceville, GA: Dake.

Henry, M. (1996). *Matthew Henry's Commentary on the Whole Bible: Complete and Unabridged in One Volume.* New Modern Edition Database, Peabody: Hendrickson Publishers.

Morgan, R. J. (2000). *Nelson's Complete Book of Stories, Illustrations, and Quotes* (electronic ed., pp. 432-433). Nashville, TN: Thomas Nelson.

CPSIA information can be obtained at www.ICGtesting.com
Printed in the USA
LVOW13*1959140314

377493LV00001B/3/P

9 781493 148516